Paired Reading, Spelling and Writing

Other titles in the Cassell Education Series:

E. Bearne, M. Styles and V. Watson (eds): *The Prose and the Passion: Children and their Reading*

J. Britton: *Literature in its Place*

H. Daniels and S. Zemelman: *A Writing Project: Training Teachers of Composition from Kindergarten to College*

C. Fox: *At the Very Edge of the Forest*

D. Gallo: *Authors' Insights: Turning Teenagers into Readers and Writers*

J. Mayer: *Uncommon Sense: Theoretical Practice in Language Education*

J. Schwartz: *Encouraging Early Literacy*

P. Shannon: *Becoming Political: Readings and Writings in the Politics of Literacy Education*

A. Stables: *An Approach to English*

M. Styles, E. Bearne and V. Watson: *After Alice: Exploring Children's Literature*

S. Tchudi and S. Tchudi: *The English/Language Arts Handbook: Classroom Strategies for Teachers*

C. Weaver: *Understanding Whole Language*

Paired Reading, Spelling and Writing

The Handbook for Teachers and Parents

KEITH TOPPING

CASSELL

Cassell
Wellington House
125 Strand
London WC2R 0BB

127 West 24th Street
New York
NY 10011

First published 1995, Reprinted 1996

British Library Cataloguing-in-Publication Data
A catalogue record for this book is available from the British Library.

Library of Congress Cataloging-in-Publication Data
Topping, Keith J.
    Paired reading, spelling and writing: the handbook for parent and peer tutoring in literacy/Keith Topping.
        p.   cm. – (Cassell practical handbook)
    Includes index.
    ISBN 0–304–32942–8: $32.00
    1. Language arts–Handbooks, manuals, etc. 2. Tutors and tutoring–Handbooks, manuals, etc. 3. Literacy–Handbooks, manuals, etc. I. Title. II. Series.
    LB1576.T67   1995   94–45161
    372.6–dc20   CIP

ISBN 0–304–32942–8 (paperback)

Typeset by York House Typographic Ltd.
Printed and bound in Great Britain by Redwood Books, Trowbridge, Wiltshire

Contents

List of Reproducibles

PAIRED READING

Part One

PRR1   Paired Reading – How To Do It
PRR2   Paired Reading Flowchart
PRR3   Paired Reading – What Are The Advantages?

Part Four (A)

PRR4   Parent-Tutored Paired Reading Planning Proforma
PRR5   Peer-Tutored Paired Reading Planning Proforma
PRR6   Home–School Diary
PRR7   Dictionary of Praise
PRR8   Paired Reading Technique Check List
PRR9   Paired Reading Evaluation Questionnaire
PRR10   Certificate of Merit
PRR11   Beyond Paired Reading Hand-out
PRR12   Overhead Masters – Paired Reading Method
PRR13   Overhead Masters – Research on Paired Reading

CUED SPELLING

Part Two

CSR1   Cued Spelling Flowchart
CSR2   Cued Spelling Diary Sheet

Part Four (B)

CSR3   Cued Spelling – How To Do It
CSR4   Mnemonic Strategies Hand-out
CSR5   Mnemonic Ideas Hand-out
CSR6   Abbreviated Cued Spelling Procedure
CSR7   Cued Spelling Evaluation Questionnaire
CSR8   Overhead Masters – Research on Cued Spelling

PAIRED WRITING

Part Three

Part Four (C)

CHAPTER 1

How to Use This Book

What This Book is About

This book is about Paired Learning in literacy – parent and peer tutoring in reading, spelling and writing.

Paired Learning tutoring is organized in pairs rather than groups. This makes it easier to organize and more effective. Pairs can be of the same or different ages, the same or different ability.

The book deals with specific structured methods, one method in each of the three areas of literacy. These are: Paired Reading, Cued Spelling and Paired Writing.

What This Book is For

This book is to help you operate Paired Reading, Cued Spelling and Paired Writing successfully.

It gives you enough description of each method, guidelines on organization and reproducible materials to enable you to run a project with a minimum of effort yet be assured of success.

It also gives you a summary of the evaluation research on these methods so you can be sure what you do has been shown to be effective.

In short, the book seeks to lower the threshold of innovation.

Although the methods described have been mainly used by natural parent and peer tutors, other kinds of tutors have been involved: volunteer parents in school and neighbourhood, non-teaching staff in schools, senior citizens, students (sometimes themselves with special needs), siblings, and so on.

The term 'tutor' will be used generically in this book to denote the person in the role of helper in the pair. The term 'tutee' will be used similarly for the member of the pair who is being helped.

These methods are designed to be flexible, durable and low cost. The possibilities are endless.

Who This Book is For

This book is written as if for an average teacher who is interested in the area but has little previous experience or specialist technical knowledge.

It is likely to be useful inside and outside schools, however. Community educators, voluntary organizations, libraries, adult education facilities, parents' groups, educational or school psychologists, teacher training colleges and in-service training agencies could all find it helpful.

All of these methods have been used successfully with adults of limited literacy as both tutees and tutors (e.g. Scoble *et al.* 1988).

Individual potential parent and peer tutors might use the 'How To Do It' chapters, in particular.

In general the style is simple and direct. However, the chapters on evaluation will be found more difficult than the rest.

How This Book is Organized

After this introductory chapter, the book is organized into four parts. Part One deals with Paired Reading, Part Two with Cued Spelling and Part Three with Paired Writing.

In each section some reproducible materials appear in the text. Additional reproducible materials will be found in Part Four, arranged into Paired Reading Reproducibles (A), Cued Spelling Reproducibles (B) and Paired Writing Reproducibles (C).

Part One on Paired Reading is about three times longer than Parts Two and Three on spelling and writing. This is for a number of reasons:

1. Reading is often considered more important than spelling or writing. More people want to run reading projects than any other sort.
2. Much more research has been done on Paired Reading than on spelling or writing.
3. A lot of the advice on organizing Paired Reading also applies to spelling and writing. There was no point in duplicating this in Parts Two and Three.

Within each of the first three Parts, a similar format will be found relating to reading (Part One), spelling (Two) and writing (Three):

What Is It?   (description of the method)
How To Organize It   (guidelines for action)
Does It Work?   (evaluation research)
How To Evaluate It   (assessing your own project)
References   (specific to that method)

It is hoped that the book will ensure success in paired learning for literacy projects. The methods described in this book are not the only ones, of course. New methods can be invented once skills and confidence have been developed.

The last chapter (11) is therefore about designing new methods of your own, to be evaluated in their turn.

How To Read This Book

If you are particularly interested in spelling or writing, you can of course dip straight into Parts Two and Three (particularly Chapters 6 and 9) to get a flavour of these methods.

However, remember that much of the detail on the organization and evaluation of Paired Reading is relevant to Cued Spelling and Paired Writing, but is not duplicated in Parts Two and Three. Before you embark on a spelling or writing project, therefore, you should read at least Chapter 3 in Part One on organizing Paired Reading, and preferably also Chapter 5 on how to evaluate Paired Reading.

In fact, to develop a complete overall understanding of paired learning in literacy, you might wish to read the whole book before starting a project in a particular area of literacy. Some people are too impatient for this, however!

History and Context

In the UK in the early 1980s, more teachers had begun to accept that parent and peer tutoring activities were 'a good thing', but felt they were much too stressed with the demands of direct classroom teaching to be able to indulge in this 'extra'.

Research by Jenny Hewison and her colleagues in London caused many to change their minds (Tizard, Schofield and Hewison 1982). The impact of a parental involvement in reading project in a disadvantaged area was compared with the effect of extra small-group help from qualified reading teachers and with regular classroom instruction alone. The parent involvement group showed far bigger gains on reading tests than the other two groups. Even more striking, the differences between the groups were still clearly evident at follow-up three years later.

Thus it became clear to teachers that to spend a little of their precious time on organizing tutoring by non-teachers was a far more cost-effective way of managing children's learning than spending all their time on direct classroom teaching.

No longer is it good enough to involve a few trusted white female middle-class parents in 'helping with reading' in school as a token gesture. The need is to involve a large cross-section of parents of all genders, races, socioeconomic classes and linguistic backgrounds. You might be able to involve grandparents, siblings, all the rest of the family, friends and neighbours and the extended peer group as well!

To achieve this, teachers must learn or develop a range of effective helping and tutoring strategies specially designed for use by non-professionals, which can be 'given away' as part of the process of empowering the community to help itself. Such tutoring methods should not be 'watered down' versions of what teachers might do in class, but must be specifically designed to capitalize on the strengths of non-professional tutors while protecting against the impact of any weaknesses such tutors may have. Such activities must complement, consolidate and extend regular classroom instruction rather than be considered a substitute for it.

Effective tutoring systems must be extremely flexible and capable of wide application by self-initiation. The aim is not just to have parents helping children. All kinds of tutoring constellations will spring up once a family has been empowered. Father might tutor son who then tutors mother who then feels able to tutor younger daughter (except on the hard bits where son takes over), for instance. In a multi-ethnic family a dual language text may permit the father to tutor the son in reading the mother tongue while the son tutors that father in reading English. Such developments advance us towards a true concept of Family Literacy.

However, this is not the place to discuss the background educational, economic, political and research issues in any depth, for this is basically a practical book. Many other volumes offer relevant background reading for those who are interested (e.g. Topping and Wolfendale 1985, Topping 1986 and 1988, Wolfendale and Topping 1995).

Current Imperatives

Literacy skills are crucially important in the world of today – for progress within the education system and for coping with life outside it.

There has been concern in many developed countries recently that literacy standards are falling, despite ever increasing expenditures on special programmes. More expensive, technical professional programmes do not seem to be the answer. For less developed countries, such exotica are impossible.

The current climate emphasizes accountability and cost-effectiveness. It is important that methods used can be demonstrated to yield substantial measurable benefits in relation to their cost of implementation. The methods in this book are of low cost and incorporate their own evaluative framework.

There is an ongoing debate about how reading should be taught in schools which resurfaces in the media from time to time. This is much exaggerated and most teachers adopt a range of eclectic methods. However, it is important that systems for tutoring by non-professionals do not interfere with learning in school. The methods in this book have been found to be entirely compatible with virtually every kind of professional teaching of literacy skills.

Some developed countries have instituted nationally prescribed curricula. There is remarkably little evidence that this actually raises standards. Sometimes these compulsory curricula are distorted or overloaded. Often they are accompanied by a compulsory testing or assessment regime. Paradoxically, the extra work involved in administering the bureaucratic system can leave teachers with less time to teach. Thus one might expect standards to fall instead of rise.

Because this book will be used throughout the world, it is inappropriate to include in it details of how paired learning methods relate precisely to particular prescribed national curriculum attainment targets in different countries. After reading the book (and preferably experiencing the operation of a project), teachers will easily be able to do this for themselves should they consider it necessary.

Future and Development

Paired Reading, Cued Spelling and Paired Writing are not the only methods you can use, of course. However, they are among the most clearly structured and best evaluated.

Hopefully you will use the design guidelines in Chapter 11 to begin to make creative adaptations to these and other methods, and perhaps eventually you will invent something completely new. Don't forget to evaluate it to make sure it works!

The focus in this book is on literacy, and this is indeed an excellent place to start, but the possibilities are endless. A great deal of work has been done on parent and peer tutoring of mathematics (see, for example, the Family Math programme by Stenmark, Thompson and Cossey 1986). Interest is spreading rapidly into other areas of the curriculum such as Science (see, for example, the Paired Science pack by Croft and Topping 1992).

References

Croft, S. and Topping, K. (1992) *Paired Science – A Resource Pack for Parents and Children.* Dundee: Centre for Paired Learning, University of Dundee.

Scoble, J., Topping, K. and Wigglesworth, C. (1988) Training family and friends as adult literacy tutors, *Journal of Reading*, **31**(5), 410–17.

Stenmark, J.K., Thompson, V. and Cossey, R. (1986) *Family Math*. Equals: Lawrence Hall of Science, Berkeley, Calif.

Tizard, J., Schofield, W.N. and Hewison, J. (1982), Collaboration between teachers and parents in assisting children's reading. *British Journal of Educational Psychology*, **52**, 1–15.

Topping, K.J. (1986) *Parents as Educators*. London: Croom Helm; Cambridge, Mass.: Brookline.

(1988) *The Peer Tutoring Handbook: Promoting Co-operative Learning*. London : Croom Helm; Cambridge, Mass.: Brookline.

Topping, K.J. and Wolfendale, S.W. (eds) (1985) *Parental Involvement In Children's Reading*. London: Croom Helm; New York: Nichols.

Wolfendale, S.W. and Topping, K.J. (eds) (1995) *Family Involvement in Literacy: Effective Partnerships in Education*. London: Cassell.

Part One
Paired Reading

CHAPTER 2

What is Paired Reading?

Paired Reading is a straightforward and enjoyable way for more able readers to help less able readers develop better reading skills. In North America it is also known as 'Duolog' Reading. The method is adaptable to any reading material, and tutees select books which are of intrinsic interest to them. Encouragement to read 'little and often' is usual.

The technique has two main aspects. Initially, tutor and tutee read out loud simultaneously in close synchrony. This is termed 'Reading Together'. The tutor adjusts their reading to the tutee's pace as necessary. The tutee must read all the words out loud correctly. Errors are corrected merely by the tutor again giving a perfect example of how to read the error word, and ensuring that the tutee repeats it correctly – then the pair continue.

The second aspect is termed 'Reading Alone' or independent reading. When the tutee feels confident enough to read a section of text unsupported, the tutee signals by a knock, nudge or other non-verbal signal for the tutor to be silent. The tutor praises the tutee for taking this initiative, and subsequently praises the tutee very regularly, especially for mastering very difficult words or spontaneously self-correcting.

When the tutee makes an error when Reading Alone, the tutor corrects this as before, by modelling and ensuring perfect repetition, and then joins back in reading simultaneously. Any word not read correctly within 4 seconds is treated as an error – the tutee is not left to struggle.

Initially, much reading is usually done simultaneously, but as the tutee improves and makes more appropriate choices of reading materials, more and more independent reading occurs. Any tendency to rush on the part of the tutee is usually resolved by consistent use of the correction procedure and visually 'pacing' the reading by pointing to each word as it is to be pronounced.

A sample 'How To Do It' leaflet for potential tutors is reproduced on p.8. This was written for parents helping their children at home. Different versions are used in peer tutoring and adult literacy. Read this leaflet now before continuing with this chapter. You may reproduce this leaflet for your own use. It is deliberately quite long and full of detail, although the readability level has been kept low. You might want to abbreviate it for your own use, or produce a simpler list of 'rules' to go with it.

For use with families or peer tutoring situations where the participants are bilingual, you might wish to have the leaflet translated into languages other than English. We have not included any examples of such translations in this book because the list of possible languages would be very long.

You might feel as if such translation would be of little use in situations where many of the bilingual population were not literate in their mother tongue. However, Paired Reading is very flexible and can be used in many ways to develop family literacy. Sometimes children will (for example) take home 'How To Do It' leaflets in two languages and/or dual-language books. This can result in an uncle using Paired

PRR1   Paired Reading – How to Do It

A Guide For Parents

Photograph: Keith Topping

Paired Reading is a very good way for parents to help with their children's reading. It works well with most children and their reading gets a lot better. Also, Paired Reading fits in very well with the teaching at school, so children don't get mixed up. Most children really like it – it helps them want to read.

What You Need

Books

First, you need books to choose from, at home or from school or the library. School will tell you about the libraries. Children can also choose newspapers, magazines or other items they want to read.

Your child should choose the book. Children learn to read better from books they like. Don't worry if it seems too difficult. In Paired Reading you help the child through the difficult bits. Your child will soon get used to picking books that aren't too difficult.

If your child becomes tired of a book, and wants to change it, that's OK. If the book is boring, it must be their own fault, of course! Perhaps they should choose more carefully next time.

Time

Try very hard to do some Paired Reading nearly every day, even if only for 5 minutes. Aim for 5 days per week. Don't do more than 15 minutes unless your child wants to carry on. Don't make children do Paired Reading when they really want to do something else.

If parents haven't got the time to do Paired Reading 5 days a week, grandmother or grandfather or older brother or sister or even friends and neighbours can help. They must all do Paired Reading in just the same way, though, or the child will get confused.

Place

Try to find a place that's quiet. Children can't read when it's noisy, or when there's lots going on. Get away from the TV, or turn it off.

Try to find a place that's comfortable. If you're not comfortable, you'll both be shifting about. Then you won't be able to look carefully at the book together.

Get close – reading together can be very warm and snuggly. You both need to be able to see the book easily – or one of you will get neck-ache!

New Ways of Helping

It's often harder for parents to learn new ways than it is for children! With Paired Reading, the hardest things for parents to get used to are:

1   When your child gets a word wrong, you just tell your child what the word says. You say the word correctly, then your child says it after you. You *don't* make the child struggle and struggle, or 'break it up' or 'sound it out'. Don't worry if you come to a word neither of you is sure about – just look it up or ask someone.

2   But don't jump in and put the word right straight away. Give the child 4 or 5 seconds to see if he/she will put it right without help. However, if your child zooms straight past a mistake without noticing it, you may have to point out the mistake a bit quicker.

3   When your child reads well, smile and show you are pleased and say 'good'. *Don't* nag and fuss about the words your child gets wrong. Give praise for: good reading of difficult words, getting all the words in a sentence right and putting wrong words right before you do (self-correction).

4   Parents often ask 'should we point at the words?' The answer is not just 'yes' or 'no'. On a difficult book, or when the child is tired or not concentrating well, pointing might help. But only do it when necessary, not all the time. And if the child can do it rather than you, that is better. Sometimes both can point together.

Talk

Show interest in the book your child has chosen. Talk about the pictures. Talk about what's in the book as your child goes through it. It's best if you talk at the end of a page or section, or your child might lose track of the story. Ask what your child thinks might happen next. Listen to your child – don't you do all the talking.

Talk is very important – it shows your interest in what the child is reading. It also checks on the child's understanding without seeming like a 'test'.

Notes

It is a help for both child and schoolteacher to keep a note of what has been read each day and how the child is progressing.

Keep a Paired Reading Diary (on a card or sheet of paper). Note down the date, what was read, for how long, who helped and any comments about how well the child did. This can be taken into school each week by the child to show the teacher – who will give more praise and write his/her own comment.

New Ways of Helping

How To Do It

Reading Together

To start with, especially when reading something which is hard for the child, you and your child both read the words out loud together. You must not go too fast. Make your speed the same as your child's. This helps the child through the difficult bits and gives a good example of how to read well.

Your child must read every word. If your child struggles and then gets it right, show you are pleased. But if your child hasn't said the word correctly in 4 or 5 seconds, just say it correctly yourself again, then let the child say it right as well, then carry on. If your child rushes past mistakes, you might have to correct them more quickly.

Make sure your child looks at the words. Especially on difficult reading, it can help if one of you points to the word you are both reading with a finger. It's best if your child will do the pointing.

Reading Alone

When you are Reading Together and your child feels confident enough, he or she might want to read a bit alone. You should agree on a way for your child to signal for you to stop Reading Together.

This could be a knock, a sign or a squeeze. Some children like to nudge you. The signal must be clear, easy to do and agreed between you before you start. (You don't want your child to have to say 'be quiet', or they will lose track of the reading.)

When the child signals, you stop reading out loud straight away, and praise the child for being confident.

When Reading Alone, sooner or later your child will struggle with a word for more than 5 seconds, or struggle and get it wrong. Then you read the word out loud correctly for your child and make sure your child says it correctly as well.

Then you both go on reading out loud *together* again, to get back into a flow. Soon your child will again feel confident enough to read alone and again signal you to be quiet. You will go on like this, switching from Reading Together to Reading Alone to give the child just as much help as they need. You will Read Together more on difficult books, less on simple books.

Try to make sure you stick to these 'Rules', at least for the first few weeks. If you don't, you may get in a muddle. Make sure you don't do each other's 'job'. The child signals to shut you up – don't you decide to go quiet when you feel like it. Also, when the child makes a mistake when Reading Alone, you must correct it and go back to Reading Together. The child might ask for you only to give them the word they got stuck on – but that's not sticking to the rules!

PRR2 Paired Reading Flowchart

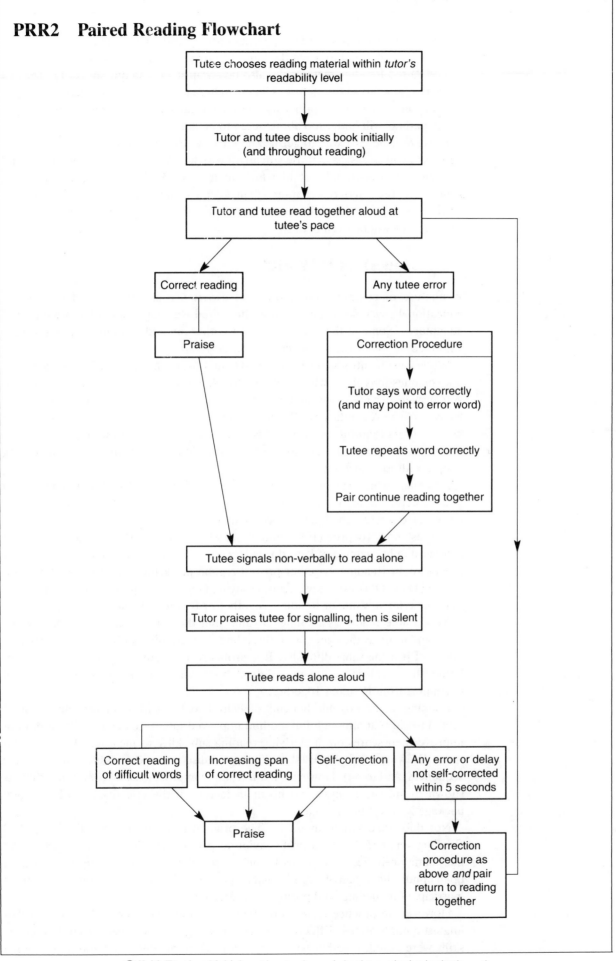

Reading to help the child and the parents learn to read the mother tongue, while the child uses the method to teach the parent to read English, for example.

The Paired Reading method can also be encapsulated on one sheet of paper in a flowchart. A chart of this nature is included here (PRR2). You may reproduce this, but remember that it this primarily intended as an *aide mémoire* for professionals. Many parents will find it too abbreviated to be helpful.

However, the best way to get to know Paired Reading is to actually *do* it. This applies to you as well as to those you might wish to tell about the method. Try to find a tame and user-friendly child who will let you practise on them. After this experience, the rest of this chapter will make much more sense. Of course, you can't always make generalizations from a sample of one, so if you can practise on two children this will be even better.

How Does It Work?

A mixture of common sense, practical experience and theory and research in educational psychology suggests that the Paired Reading method has a number of advantages. Some of these are common to other methods for non-teachers to help with reading, but some are specific to Paired Reading.

When you are introducing the method to new users, the more curious of them may ask you questions about why the Paired Reading rules are the way they are. To help you answer such questions, and for your own information, you may wish to read the hand-out 'The Advantages of Paired Reading' on pp. 13. You may reproduce this to give to tutors (and tutees!) if you wish. However, emphasize that it is an optional hand-out for those who are interested, otherwise you run the risk of drowning people with too much information.

You might want to go on to consider the research on why Paired Reading works in greater depth. Some of this research is summarized in Chapter 4. However, the answers from research alone are not clear cut.

For instance, Toepritz (1982) noted that while the proportion of Reading Alone increased in her sample of Paired Readers over time, neither this nor the degree of synchrony in Reading Together proved a good predictor of post-project gains on reading tests. Of course, this might be saying more about the value of reading tests than the relative value of Reading Together or Reading Alone.

Young able readers sometimes assume that they are expected to Read Alone more and more as they get better at reading. In fact, this is only true if they stick to books of just the same difficulty. It is probably more advantageous if, as they get better, they tackle more and more difficult books and therefore still need a good deal of support from Reading Together.

Looking at the possible benefits of Paired Reading from another angle, Scott (1983) noted that although the method improved tutees' reading ability, it did not improve their scores on 'underlying reading sub-skills' as measured by the Aston Index (Newton *et al.*, 1979) (skills like visual discrimination, auditory memory for sequences, and so on). However, it *did* result in improved use of contextual clues as shown by miscue analysis. So no main factors in the effectiveness of the total package have yet been isolated.

Nor does theory help us much. The original theoretical conception of Paired Reading was largely based on behavioural psychology. Some educators have an automatic prejudice against this branch of social science. Please read on with an open mind! The design of Paired Reading particularly stemmed from the concepts of 'participant modelling' and positive reinforcement.

However, in practice it was soon found that the technique had strong psycho-linguistic implications. Effects on tutees' reading style and background language skills were noted, together with improvements in the emotional and motivational aspects of reading (for more detail see Chapter 4). It is clear from evaluation

PRR3 Paired Reading – What are the Advantages?

1 Children are encouraged to pursue their own interests in reading material. They have more enthusiasm from reading about their own favourite things, and so try harder. Paired Reading gives them as much support as they need to read whatever book they choose.

2 Children are more in control of what's going on – instead of having reading crammed into them, they make decisions themselves in the light of their own purposes (e.g. about choice of books, going on longer than 10 minutes and going onto Reading Alone).

3 There is no failure – it is impossible not to say a word correctly within 5 seconds or so.

4 Paired Reading is very flexible – the child decides how much support is necessary according to the current level of interest, mood, degree of tiredness, amount of confidence, difficulty of the books, and so on.

5 The child gets lots of praise – it's much nicer to be told when you're doing well, instead of just being moaned at when you go wrong.

6 There's lots of emphasis of understanding – getting the meaning out of the words – and that's what reading is all about. It's no use being able to read the words out loud mechanically without following the meaning.

7 Paired Reading gives continuity – it eliminates stopping and starting to 'break up' difficult words. Doing that often leaves children having forgotten the beginning of the sentence by the time they get to the end. With Paired Reading it is easier for children to make sensible guesses at new words, based on the meaning of the surrounding words.

8 During Reading Together, a child can learn (by example) to read with expression and the right pacing – e.g. by copying how the adult pauses at punctuation, or gives emphasis to certain words.

9 Children are given a perfect example of how to pronounce difficult words, instead of being left to work it out themselves and then perhaps thinking their own half-right efforts are actually 100 per cent correct.

10 When doing Paired Reading, children get a bit of individual peaceful, private attention from their parents, which they might not otherwise have had. There is some evidence that just giving children more attention can actually improve their reading.

11 Paired Reading increases the amount of sheer practice at reading children get. Because children are supported through books, they get through them faster. The number of books read in a week goes up, the number of words children look at in a week goes up, and more words stick in the child's memory.

12 Paired Reading gives parents a clear, straightforward and enjoyable way of helping their children – so no-one gets confused, worried or bad-tempered about reading.

SO CHILDREN HAVE MORE INTEREST, CONFIDENCE AND UNDERSTANDING.

research repeatedly showing massive increases in comprehension that Paired Reading is certainly not just improving mechanical skills.

Bushell *et al.* (1982) noted that during Paired Reading fragmentation of the reading process by over-focusing on difficult words is much reduced. This creates the opportunity to use contextual clues and aids prediction of both upcoming grammatical structure and overall meaning. However, it may well be true that the factors of modelling, prompting and reinforcement embodied in the original design by Roger Morgan (1976) also have an effect. Heath's work (1981) showed that the positive effects of the technique are not solely due to the reinforcement aspect.

Whatever the design origins, Paired Reading is now acknowledged to have wide-ranging effects which are considered desirable by virtually all of the many different schools of thought on the teaching of reading. It is likely that different tutees benefit via different pathways or combinations of pathways. So attempts to find out which single route has the biggest effect for the largest number of children are probably only of academic interest.

Where Does It Fit?

Although Paired Reading, named as such, came into being in the mid–1970s, it had certainly been foreshadowed. While it might seem novel to the parents of current schoolchildren, their grandparents would have been entirely familiar with group reading of favourite Bible passages in synchrony. Likewise, speech therapists have for some time used the technique of 'shadowing' with stammerers – providing a continuous model and prompt of fluent speech.

In the United States, a number of approaches showing some of the features of Paired Reading have been developed over the years (Wisner 1988, Topping 1990). These include 'Reading-While-Listening', the 'Lap Method', 'Shadow Reading', 'Duet Reading', 'Assisted Reading', 'Prime-O-Tec', 'Talking Books' and the more fearsomely named 'Neurological Impress Method'. Few of these were designed for use by non-teachers, however. Nevertheless, no single feature of Paired Reading is at all new. The effectiveness of the technique lies in the assembly and coherence of its elements – the total engineered 'package'. The whole is more than the sum of its parts.

Of the various elements of Paired Reading, the positive effect of adult modelling pure and simple on children's reading had been noticed elsewhere (e.g. Smith 1979). In this study, the adult read the first section of text fluently and the tutee carried on unaided from where the adult left off. The tutee's reading ability was even further raised with the introduction of a correction procedure for errors involving adult modelling of the correct response. Still greater improvements were found when the tutee commenced reading back at the start of the text, having had a 'preview' with adult modelling.

As early as 1968 Neville had noted that listening to a reading or recording of a text while following it visually helped increase fluency. In 1975 a further study by Neville of 180 children of normal reading ability showed that the slowest of three speeds of simultaneous listening with silent reading resulted in the highest level of comprehension. This 'pacing effect' seemed even more marked in a small sample of 'remedial' readers, and seemed to be more prominent among boys.

Research by Johnson (1982) found boys had very poor recall performance compared to girls on a silent reading task. This was in contrast with the equal recall performance of boys and girls after listening to and after orally reading a message. Wilkinson (1980) also reported that simultaneous listening and reading facilitated comprehension, even with highly skilled readers. Horowitz and Samuels (1985) found little difference in *listening* comprehension between good and poor readers.

It seems that simultaneous reading and listening, as in 'Reading Together', frees the struggling reader from a preoccupation with laborious decoding and enables other reading strategies to come into play. If the 'limited processing capacity' (Curtis 1980) of the remedial reader is totally devoted to accurate word recognition or phonic analysis and synthesis, no processing capacity is left to deploy other strategies, such as using contextual clues. Hutson, Cowger and Wallbrown (1980) and Potter (1982) both provided evidence that weak readers are usually less able, and consequently less willing, to use psycholinguistic strategies, and tend to depend heavily on a phonic approach.

Paradoxically, teachers tend to reinforce this over-dependence, not only by assuming that given sufficient phonic nuts and bolts the tutee will spontaneously prove able to assemble a machine, but also by interrupting weak readers to give phonic cues far more often in proportion to mistakes made than they do with competent readers. This constant interruption further reduces the contextual clues available to the reader (Allington 1980, Shake 1986). It is perhaps unsurprising that weak readers tend to display characteristics of learned helplessness (Butkowsky and Willows 1980). These features of reading failure are precisely those which Paired Reading seems effective in remedying.

Paired Reading can do a lot of good, but equally important is that it seems to do little harm. Paired Reading at home lies down perfectly happily with a school reading curriculum based on look-and-say, phonics, language experience, pictograms, precision teaching, direct instruction or any other kind of approach. Indeed, there is considerable advantage in home and school pursuing different approaches, since Paired Reading is complementary to all, and is a labour-intensive method which is often impossible to carry through consistently in school.

Those who wish to read more about the theoretical underpinnings of Paired Reading and its connections with the wider literature on how children learn to read should consult Topping and Lindsay (1992b).

A Warning

From what you have already read, you will now be clear that 'Paired Reading' is a specific name for a specific technique. It is *not* any old thing that two people feel like doing together with a book.

Unfortunately the name has become too widely misused. You will often meet people who say 'Oh, yes, we do that Paired Reading'. When you actually look at what they are doing you often find that it is nothing like the specific method we have described above. This is why it was renamed 'Duolog' Reading in North America.

So take care – just because you use the same name as someone else, it doesn't mean that the same ideas or practice are necessarily attached to the label. Take time to make sure that you are actually talking the same language.

Even more problematic is the name 'Shared Reading'. This is sometimes used interchangeably with 'Paired Reading', quite wrongly. In fact, there are three quite different meanings of the term 'Shared Reading' in use, all of which are different from Paired Reading. Further details of the definitions and differences will be found in Topping (1986). This book is about *proper* Paired Reading.

You will also encounter opinions about Paired Reading which are based on wild misconceptions. It was once accused in the media of being a communist plot. Honestly. The much overblown debate about the 'right' method of teaching reading, which recurs every few years, is relevant here. The eccentric attack on Paired Reading referred to was made on the grounds that it did not have a high phonic content. Certainly Paired Reading tutors are asked not to give phonic prompts when tutees stumble on a word. However, in the five-second pause, tutees have the opportunity to apply whatever phonic skills they may have learned through regular classroom instruction or elsewhere. That is, the phonic skills they have, not the phonic skills their tutor thinks they should have. However, if the tutee cannot deploy their phonic skills within the five-second pause, the word is supplied in order to sustain extraction of meaning without undue stress.

Phonic prompting, tutoring or teaching can quickly become tedious and are easy to do badly. The Paired Reading method proceeds on the assumption that phonic instruction is best left in the hands of the expert in the classroom. It makes no prescription about what processes should go on inside the child's head. It merely manages surface reading behaviour so that success is guaranteed and practice is positive. Within this supportive scaffolding, the child is free to use whatever reading strategies are effective for them for that word at that moment in time. The analogy to learning to ride a bicycle with the supporting hand of a parent or peer on the frame but not on your body is an apt one.

The whole debate about whether national reading standards are rising, falling or staying the same is also relevant here. Paired Reading raises scores on reading tests – of comprehension as well as accuracy. Chapter 4 evidences this quite clearly. The method has been better evaluated than many other educational procedures. But there are dangers. One is that a school worried about its reading standards in this era of competitive comparison might launch a Paired Reading project to help resolve the problem. If the effect of that was to deflect attention from any weaknesses in the organization of reading teaching by the professionals in the school, parent and peer tutors would be justifiably aggrieved. If standards do rise, the credit should be shared.

The moral of this tale is: whenever you hear Paired Reading attacked, ask the complainants to define their terms and state their hidden agenda.

CHAPTER 3

How to Organize Paired Reading

This chapter is in two parts. The first part considers organization for parent tutoring. The second part looks at the differences when organizing peer tutoring. Each of the two parts is linked with its own 'Planning Proforma'. These are action check lists on which to write your planning decisions as you make them. They are intended to ensure that you have thought of everything and can't go wrong! You might want to look at these in the course of reading this chapter. You will find them in Part Four Section A of this book, Parent Tutoring numbered PRR4 and Peer Tutoring numbered PRR5.

Organizing for Parent Tutoring

Not all teachers are happy about parental involvement in children's reading. Those who are not may feel that the control of the learning process should continue to reside with the professionals. Other teachers may feel that the parents of children at their school would not be competent, literate or committed enough to use the technique properly. Both these views are wrong. You should, however, be aware that you might meet resistance as you set about organizing your project, and it is as well to have your counter arguments already marshalled.

In the first place, education must have relevance to life after school, if it is to have any enduring value at all. There is little point in schools teaching children to read, if the children never read outside the school boundary. Teaching reading hopefully includes developing the desire to read in children, and the evidence strongly suggests that parental example has much more influence in this respect than anything teachers can do.

In any case, many parents will try to 'help' their children at home regardless of the school's view on the matter. If the school offers no guidance to parents, many harmful practices which do indeed conflict with, and sabotage, the teaching in school may develop in homes. Furthermore, the extent to which teachers actually control children's learning is doubtful. Certainly, teachers will carefully control the complexity and sequence of the educational experiences to which they expose children, but how the children respond to these and other external experiences is up to them. Children are likely to be learning a great deal incidentally, including from other children, during the course of any experience.

Parental involvement may arouse feelings of insecurity in the teaching profession. If parents start teaching children to read, it may be thought, doesn't that imply that teachers are redundant? This is far from being the case, of course. Children will still need sophisticated teaching in language, phonic skills and grammar in school, which few parents could effectively undertake. Paired Reading does not eliminate the necessity for this kind of teaching, but does enable the teacher to delegate some of the more straightforward aspects of helping children learn to read to the parents. Paired Reading is about maximizing positive practice.

Freed from the necessity to 'hear children read' with the same degree of frequency, teachers can devote more time to refining the more technical aspects of their professional work. Paired Reading complements the work teachers do in school, rather than replicating or replacing it. Also, parents need professional training and support if they are to learn to use the technique of Paired Reading properly – and teachers are clearly best placed to provide this.

If a school has a few hours of teaching time to devote to helping children with reading, the evidence strongly suggests it will be much more cost-effective to use that time to train and support parents in the Paired Reading technique, rather than offer the children fragmentary and irregular direct teaching from a professional.

But surely the parents of the children who most need help will be those who are least likely to cooperate, you might say. To some extent this might be true, but experience proves it is actually very difficult to predict which parent will learn the method quickest and cooperate best. A school's view of some parents as 'inadequate' or 'uncooperative' may merely reflect the extent to which the school has already frozen the parents out of participation in their children's education.

Most professional groups can be suspicious, defensive and desirous of preserving their secret skills and mystique, and teachers are no exception. It is true that parents whose own school experiences were unhappy will have their own resistance to overcome if they are to be able to help their children, but surely schools should do all in their power to prevent continuation of the cycle of disadvantage with the next generation. Like children, parents should not be underestimated. The warmth of the reception given to parents by the school will be a crucial factor. Where a school already enjoys good relationships with the community, the establishment of a Paired Reading scheme will be much easier.

Low levels of parental literacy may not prove as large a problem as might be expected. The only real necessity is that one of the parents is a little more competent in reading than the child in question. Even if neither parent is literate, there may be a grandparent or elder brother or sister who is able to learn the technique and use it regularly. The latter may often apply in families where English is not the mother tongue, where the literacy in English of the parents may not be good even if their capacity in oral English is adequate. Different ethnic minority groups respond differentially well to Paired Reading. They are as different from each other as they are from the 'natives' of the country.

Neither should it be assumed that Paired Reading is a purely 'remedial' technique. It has proved useful with children who have made a start with reading, but do not seem to be progressing, perhaps owing to emotional complications. Likewise, the child termed 'dyslexic' may benefit. But beyond these, some schools have adopted the method for use across whole year groups and age ranges – for all children of all levels of ability whose parents are interested. The method is useful with children who are complete non-starters at reading at any age. For young children, Paired Reading is a logical development from parents' reading stories to the children.

So how do we set it up? A number of factors should be taken into consideration when planning the establishment of a parent-tutored Paired Reading project. These can be grouped under the headings: Context, Objectives, Materials, Recruitment, Training, Support and Monitoring, Feedback, Evaluation.

Context

The first and perhaps major question is: Who has the time, energy and commitment to set it up? In any school, a minimum of two enthusiastic teachers is necessary. A single teacher who tries to set up a scheme in isolation from the rest of the staff will find it a struggle, especially if the Head Teacher is barely tolerant of the proposal.

Second, consideration should be given to the nature of the school's catchment area, the degree of reading difficulty common to the pupils, the existence of minority groups whose needs may be slightly different and the existing relationships between school and community. You also need to consider geographical ease of access to the school for parent meetings. From this will come an estimate of how much time and energy needs pouring into the project to ensure its success, or (to put it another way) how hard it is going to be.

Next, some thought about the organizational context of the school is required. What are reading standards in the school like generally? If they are alarmingly low, it may be unwise to launch a Paired Reading project, if all it serves to do is conceal fundamental flaws in the organization of reading teaching in school. Likewise, if there is division among the teaching staff, a Paired Reading project could be used as a scapegoat for one of the factions, who might be happy to see the project fail. It is worth pondering whether there are any other social or political factors which may sabotage the project.

Objectives

It is important to be clear about your objectives, since if you are not clear what outcome(s) you are hoping for, you will not be able to tell whether the project was a success or not. However, life is full of surprises, so you may find some positive effects which you had not expected.

At this point, a suitable target group of children can be identified, in terms of ages, reading level, class membership and numbers involved. There is a lot to be said for building in some success for a school's first experience with Paired Reading, so it would be unwise to target a large number of children with severe reading difficulty to start with. An initial target group of a modest number of children of a range of reading ability is probably the best bet.

Do not pick a few children from many different classes. It is best if the target group already have a good deal of social contact in the school. If you can involve a significant number in the project, the children will begin to encourage and reinforce each other. Deliberately try to create a group social ethos which is positive towards the project. If children feel isolated by being labelled as Paired Readers, they might feel picked on and stigmatized by the adults who selected them. Including a wider range of reading ability in the project helps to avoid any playground mythology that Paired Reading is for the backward. In this context you will also need to think about how the project might relate to the school's existing programmes for teaching reading.

Next, some clarity must be achieved on the nature of the Paired Reading project to be undertaken. Is it to be a straightforward attempt to involve parents with their own children? Or would you prefer to start with something a bit less ambitious and more under the school's control, such as a scheme involving a few volunteer parents who come into school to do Paired Reading with children to whom they are not related? Such volunteers need not be parents themselves, for they could equally be sprightly senior citizens or other members of the local community.

A scheme involving the natural parents of the target children is the best, however, since all kinds of positive side effects and spin-offs accrue in this situation, in addition to improvements in reading skill.

So what sort of gains might be expected from the project? Are you hoping just for improvements in reading – accuracy? comprehension? fluency? Are you also looking for improved attitudes toward reading? Or improved attitudes to the self – better confidence, self-esteem and so on? Or are you looking to extend the children's experience of reading – to different material, different places, higher levels of difficulty? Or are you using the project for other purposes, such as to improve home–school relationships generally, give the school a better image locally, increase the enrolment rate, etc.?

You do need to be honest about your objectives. Of course, you may find that different teachers who are involved actually have different objectives for the project. Subsequently one could consider the project a success while the other considered it a failure. Without honesty about objectives you can get in a terrible tangle.

Materials

If you are following the Paired Reading 'rules' to the letter, you will give children completely free choice of reading materials. However, with very young or very slow readers, or those whose parents are of limited literacy, you might want to set a readability ceiling below which the children have free choice.

In view of the accelerated rate of reading which is associated with the Paired Reading technique, the availability of reading material must be scrutinized. This raises questions about the existing quantity, quality, variety and means of access. The children's demand for reading material *interesting to them* might double or treble. The demand for non-fiction is especially likely to increase.

If the school has an existing system for books to be taken home, this may need extending to *all* books in the school, including reading schemes, supplementary readers, other fiction and non-fiction, books in classrooms and in the school library, and so on. The local Libraries Service may be helpful in providing a special loan collection of attractive books just for use by the Paired Reading children. Alternatively, you might be able to siphon off a 'special collection' for the Paired Readers from sources within school.

Information about access to local libraries should be gathered and made available to parents. You may wish to incorporate a visit to the local public library as part of your project. All kinds of reading materials should be displayed in an accessible and stimulating way. You may be able to organize other literacy related activities during the project. The children will soon start recommending books to each other and you may wish to give them a noticeboard or other way of communicating their views – but don't make it too much like hard work!

The existing system for recording loans of books should be scrutinized. A Paired Reading project will usually greatly increase loan rates and put heavy strain on the current recording system, especially if it is rather unwieldy or elaborate. You might wish to streamline the system, devolve some of the work and responsibility on to the children, or have volunteer parents operate the loan arrangements.

Recruitment

Assuming that a group meeting in school for parents is to be a feature of the project at some stage, communication must be established with the target parents prior to any request to attend a meeting. Preparatory information can be communicated verbally, at Open Evenings, and in writing in conjunction with school reports. Every opportunity to establish informal personal contact with the parents must be taken. Parents will want some idea as to why their children have been chosen, especially if the school considers their children to have reading difficulty, but has never made this clear to the parents before. If you have chosen some target children at random for 'experimental' purposes, you will need to tell their parents of this.

You may wish to raise your public profile by using posters or the local media. Subsequently, letters of invitation to the initial meeting can be distributed, hopefully not in a predictable, boring or pompous format. There should be a reply slip to give you an idea of how many to expect. A final reminder just before the meeting is likely to be necessary. It is often effective to whip up enthusiasm in the children at school, and hope that they transmit some of this to their parents. There may be some value in having children write out their own letters of invitation, or develop the format of the letter as a group project. Final reminders and/or persuasion via telephone will be possible with some parents.

If there are children you see as being in particular need of involvement in your project, you may wish to make special efforts to contact their parents beforehand. Perhaps a preparatory home visit would be a good investment of time if you have any at all to spare. This will be especially true in families where the parents are of restricted literacy or speak English as a second or third language.

However, as has been said before, do not worry if not all the 'worst' cases in the neighbourhood do not get involved in your first project. It is very important that your first is successful. Once you achieve that, the good news will ripple around the community over garden fences and you will find subsequent recruitment becomes easier and easier, with 'difficult' families more and more represented, as momentum gathers.

Training

Next, ensure that the project coordinators actually know what they are talking about. They need to have not only read about Paired Reading but actually to have tried it out – preferably with a few different children. You can't talk sensibly to parents about it until you have done it yourself.

A live demonstration, or failing that a demonstration on video, is highly desirable. Contact with other local schools already using the technique, or with the local School Psychological Service or Advisory Service, may provide such an opportunity. Following this, practice is necessary. The project organizers should seize any opportunity to practise the technique on a range of children – preferably not the intended target children.

It is always helpful if other staff in the school or other project centre are briefed about the method and the project. You may, therefore, wish to run a brief in-service training session for your colleagues to ensure some minimal level of consistent awareness exists among the professionals before proceeding further. Try to ensure there is an opportunity for doubts and reservations to be tabled and discussed. Reproducible overhead masters to help you with this will be found in Part Four Section A (PRR12 and 13).

In setting the date for your 'launch' meeting with parents and children, you need to establish the length of the initial period of the project – 6, 8 or 10 weeks. Shorter 'trial' periods are probably better with younger or less motivated children. Fit this neatly into a term or semester, so the active period is not broken by a long holiday or vacation. You might also need to avoid other major conflicting or disruptive events.

This initial commitment creates clear expectations for tutees and tutors. It also ensures that the majority use the technique frequently enough to become both fluent and practised in it, and also to see a significant change in the reading ability of the tutee, which should reinforce the tutors into continuing their use of the technique in the longer term.

The structure of the training for the parent and child participants must now be carefully delineated. Always have parents and children at training meetings, so both receive exactly the same message and can practise straight away. An evening meeting may be necessary if working parents are to attend. You might have to run two parallel meetings, one during the school day and one in the evening. Most suitable times and days must be established. Avoid days with major ball games or popular TV programmes! One meeting may suffice and minimizes parental costs of attending, or two could be considered to teach the two phases of the method separately. Consider whether you should, and can, provide transport and/or child-minding facilities.

You will need to identify one major meeting room and some additional more private practice spaces. It is very important that the children have already chosen books with which to practise, otherwise there will be a delay and melee while they rush about choosing. Their classteacher should have had them choose two books prior to the meeting for practice purposes. Left to their own devices, many will choose books too easy for the appropriate practice of Reading Together, so check that they have at least one book which is above their independent readability level.

A warm, welcome and informal atmosphere to put everyone at their ease is essential. You may wish to offer refreshments, but do not attempt to do this in the middle of the meeting. At the beginning is OK, but at the end is best. A brief introduction can set the national and local scene, outline the objectives of the project and summarize positive evaluation results from the research literature.

Some 'lecturing' about the method and its effectiveness is inevitable, but long words and jargon must be avoided, as must appearing patronizing. A video or live role play between teachers of 'How *Not* To Do It' may be useful to break the ice, while making some very pertinent points. Written instructions about the method, perhaps accompanied by check lists or summary guidelines for ready reference, will be necessary. Readability should be kept low. The standard of production should be good to demonstrate that the project is important and professionally run. Do not give out written materials before talking – they should merely serve as a reminder of what everyone has learned.

A demonstration of how to do Paired Reading is essential, either on video, or by role play between adults, or by a live demonstration with a cooperative and socially robust child tutored by a teacher. (At subsequent meetings, parents and children who have already experienced success with the technique will be available to give demonstrations and/or offer testimonials.)

The advantages of the video are that it is easily seen and heard by a large group, which real live children may not be. Very brief clips of Reading Together and Reading Alone can be inserted at relevant points in your presentation. Choose 2–3 minute clips relevant to your audience. Never show a whole video – you will bore people. Make sure the equipment is working adequately for use with a large group and that you have your selected clips cued up, with any counter readings synchronized to the specific machine you are using. The video has the advantage of being predictable – well, more predictable than child actors! Perhaps most importantly, it can also be criticized, so you can pause and make teaching points about what has and has not happened in the sequence shown.

You may wish to try making your own video. There are great advantages in having video demonstration by local people in local accents. It helps to foster a sense of belonging and ownership. Bear in mind how the video is to be used, as detailed above. Do not try to compete with network television. You can't. Do not try to make a stand-alone, self-explanatory programme. It won't work and will bore people.

All you need is a few short clips of Reading Together and Reading Alone, perhaps with participants of different ages, reading levels, gender and ethnic origin, so you can choose the most appropriate for any particular audience and intersperse them with talk. However, do not underestimate the difficulty of achieving this.

Pay careful attention to obtaining good audio. Remember people rarely do for the camera what they did in rehearsal. Fathers may be particularly difficult to recruit as movie stars. There is also the problem that if your actors do Paired Reading badly, you will not be able to 'criticize' the poor aspects for teaching purposes in front of their friends and neighbours at subsequent showings. Video role play by teachers of 'How *Not* To Do It' is valuable for this.

At this stage of the training meeting, it is very valuable to encourage all parents and children to actually practise the method before leaving. If you express this as a standard expectation, the vast majority of parents cooperate happily. If parents have not brought their children, substitute children or adult role play can be used. The teachers or other professionals can then circulate and offer praise and/or further guidance as necessary. This monitoring of practice does require a high staffing ratio – one professional is unlikely to be able to visit more than five families during a brief practice period.

Pairs who are doing well can be praised and left to continue. Pairs who are struggling may need one of three levels of further coaching. First, give further verbal advice. If that doesn't work, try joining in with the Reading Together to model the pacing and intonation through triad reading. Third, if all else fails, take the book and demonstrate with the child yourself, then pass the book back and let the pair continue with level one and two support.

Lastly, it is helpful to gather people back together and deal briefly with any other points of organization – where the children can obtain books, how often, how the monitoring system will work, what to do if there are problems, and so on. *After* the practice is the time for any questions, although many parents will prefer to ask you questions individually during your visits at practice time.

Parents and children could be asked for a verbal or written decision as to whether they wish to be included in the project or not, and possibly also be asked to indicate preferences for alternative forms of follow-up support. Virtually no parents ever refuse. The whole meeting should generate a lively, exciting aura, so people feel they are part of a new experimental venture. Some projects hand out badges at launch meetings to foster a sense of belonging – and to turn children into walking advertisements for subsequent projects!

Support and monitoring

A most useful minimal form of monitoring is a home–school recording system. Children and parents make a note of what and how much is read each night and the child takes the record sheet into school each week for the teacher to add further comments and praise. A reproducible form suitable for this purpose will be found in Part Four Section A (PRR6).

This form asks parent or child to record what has been read, for how long (so they can be praised for doing more than the minimum or restrained if they are doing too much), and with whom (so we can see how many different tutors and estimate the risk of inconsistent procedure). There is a space each day for the tutor to write some (hopefully positive) comment about the tutee's performance. Of course we do not expect Paired Reading to actually happen every day, only five days out of seven.

Some tutors soon run out of good things to say. To help those with a restricted vocabulary of praise the Dictionary of Praise was devised. This will be found in Part Four Section A (PRR7) and may be reproduced. There is also a space for the teacher or other professional to write some positive comment each week, which serves to encourage both parent and child.

The record form offers a means to keep home and school in touch and give the child a double dose of praise from two very important sources. It also, of course, serves as a three-way accountability measure. While the teacher will see if the parents aren't doing their bit, the parents will see if the teacher hasn't bothered to sign the card or model good quality, written praise. It can also serve as an emergency signalling system – if things aren't working out at home, a cry for help can be written on the card.

The easiest method for using diary cards is probably to have them colour coded by weeks, so it is very easy to see if one goes astray. When the week's card has been seen by the teacher, a new colour card for the ensuing week can be issued which can be stapled on to the old one. The cards thus form an accumulating record of achievement. However, do not underestimate the teacher time involved in checking the cards weekly. If you have fifteen Paired Readers in your class and you spend five minutes each per week discussing their diary cards, that amounts to an hour and a quarter per week!

Naturally, there will be some children and families for whom this relatively lightweight form of monitoring will not suffice. You may wish to schedule meetings between teachers and individual families in school to resolve any difficulties which arise, or larger group 'booster' meetings for further practice and mutual feedback. Families can be asked to rate their own performance against check lists of good practice. A reproducible specimen check list for this purpose will be found in Part Four Section A (PRR8).

Visits to the homes of particularly needy families by teachers are very valuable in developing home–school relationships. They also enable professionals to see the family doing Paired Reading in their usual way in their own familiar context. The check list (PRR8) is often used by teachers in this situation. However, such visits are very expensive in teacher time and should be reserved for the most needy cases, even though all children and many parents might like them. Where home visiting is possible, a visit within the first two weeks of operation of the project is highly desirable. A source of funding for reimbursing teacher travelling expenses might need locating.

Some form of follow-up support and monitoring for the coordinating teacher(s) is also highly desirable, especially where the project is a first attempt or the project leader is professionally isolated. Support may come from mentors within school, or perhaps better from some external consultant such as the school psychologist. Teachers should pro-actively recruit support of this kind.

Feedback

Parental involvement in children's reading is a collaborative venture between the three main participants – teachers, parents and children. If the initiative is to become self-sustaining and grow, all three parties need to feel valued and appreciated, consulted and empowered.

It is, therefore, important that after the stipulated 'trial' or experimental period of Paired Reading, parents and children share their views on the success or otherwise of the venture. At this point they also need to make their own decision about where they are going to go from here. Some families may choose to go on doing Paired Reading five (or seven!) days a week, some may wish to go on doing it but only three days a week, some may wish to try another kind of approach to reading at home, some may wish to try parental involvement in another curriculum area such as spelling (see Part Two of this book), while a very few might wish to stop altogether.

Feedback meetings may include parents and children all together or separately. More mature children may cope well with the former (remember Paired Reading makes them more confident!), but younger children should perhaps have a separate simultaneous meeting at which their views are gathered by a professional. Parents and children can then meet up to hear the professionals' summary of both sets of views. You may expect to hear many contradictory opinions expressed at such meetings. Remember that it is important that they have a chance to give their views – that itself has valuable effects. You may end up feeling that you cannot possibly follow all the advice given about making 'improvements', however!

The feedback meeting can be much more relaxed and informal than the training meeting. The professionals should give their feedback to the parents first, modelling the appropriate behaviour. Urge those who are usually quiet in meetings to offer a comment, however brief. If you have evaluation results for your project at this time you could report those in summary to the parents. Do not give data about individual children. Specific numbers are probably best avoided even in private discussion with the pair themselves.

You will want to celebrate the success of the children, parents and school. Schools have their own styles in these matters. Some form of certificate is often well received, or perhaps an even grander badge. Very often parents will appreciate these as well! A reproducible certificate for this purpose will be found in Part Four Section A (PRR10).

If you wish to discuss possible modifications to the Paired Reading procedure for those pairs who feel ready to move on, the reproducible hand-out Beyond Paired Reading (PRR11) might be useful.

Evaluation

There is considerable virtue in building-in some form of evaluation for the initial 'experimental' period of the project. This is especially true where the project is a first for the school. There may have been positive evaluation results from many other projects nationally, but that doesn't necessarily mean you made it work right there where you are!

The evaluation of Paired Reading projects is considered in detail in Chapter 5 – How To Evaluate Paired Reading.

Summary

Stages in the development of a Paired Reading project:

1   Identify project leaders
2   Consider context factors
3   Determine objectives
4   Identify target group
5   Identify manpower source
6   Arrange book availability
7   Familiarization of project leaders
8   Recruitment of parental interest
9   Organization of training meeting
10   Evaluation pretesting
11   Run training meeting
12   Organize support and monitoring system
13   Evaluation post-testing
14   Feedback to participants
15   Maintenance and further development

Naturally, the first project a school runs is the most difficult and consumes the most energy. Once the teachers involved are familiar with the procedure, and all the required materials are to hand, the project can be run for subsequent target groups with much less hard work involved.

Organizing for Peer Tutoring

Many of the planning considerations relevant for parent tutoring are also relevant for peer tutoring. If you have turned directly to this section you should go to the beginning of the chapter and read the whole. What follows largely covers the different or additional planning aspects for peer tutoring. These are divided into subsections: Context and objectives, Reading materials, Selection and matching of children, Organization of contact, Training, Support and monitoring, Feedback, Evaluation.

Context and objectives

Contextual strengths and weakness will need assessing for a peer tutor project in a way very similar to that for a parent-tutor project. Although it is possible to operate a peer-tutor reading project entirely within the confines of your own classroom, some support from colleagues inside or outside school is highly desirable to maximize the chance of a successful first project. At the very least, the agreement of the Head Teacher to the project is essential. If this is a new venture for the school, advice and support from teacher colleagues in other, more experienced, local schools or specialist advisory agencies should be sought.

Careful consideration should be given to potential problems which are specific to your individual school. There may be difficulties with a large proportion of ethnic minority pupils, or with massive reading problems in a particular age group, or a problem of the pupils being so alienated from the aims of institutional education that initially they feel unable to play the part of tutor comfortably. If you feel that reading standards in the school are, in general, lower than they should be, take especial care. It is very important that peer-tutor projects are not used to compensate for, and thereby perhaps disguise, fundamental weaknesses in the professional teaching of reading within a school.

It is also important that teachers do not see in peer tutoring a means of giving children extra reading practice while they remain under the direct supervision and control of a professional as an alternative to the possibly more challenging develop-ment of involving the natural parents of the children in this exercise at home. Natural parents acting as reading helpers at home have great strengths, as well as weaknesses, in this role which are different to those of either peer tutors or professional teachers.

Different teachers will run peer-tutor projects for very different purposes, and a success for one teacher could be construed as a failure by another teacher with different objectives. Objectives do need to be realistic.

It is reasonable to expect both tutors and tutees to show increased accuracy and fluency of reading, better comprehension and increased confidence and love of literature. It is not reasonable to expect a brief project to completely resolve a long-standing reading problem in the school.

Peer-tutor projects often include social gains among their objectives. Thus in a cross-age project, one aim may be to increase a sense of cohesiveness and caring between older and younger children. In a project which matches children across genders and races, familiarization may also yield social benefits.

Peer tutoring should also be characterized by explication of objectives for the tutors. Well-organized peer tutoring should involve 'learning by teaching' for the tutors, who should also gain in reading skill, attitudes, social integration and self esteem. If you cannot specify valid educational objectives for the tutors, you are merely 'using' them, and their parents will rightly object to this.

Reading materials

Teachers should resist the temptation to control the readability of the material used to the tutee's current independent readability level. To do this is usually to create a situation which fails to stretch the tutee and runs the risk of boring the tutor. However, the readability of the material should certainly have a ceiling placed upon it at the *tutor's* independent reading level. Avoid at all costs the tutee presenting the tutor with failure, or the generation of confusion by both children losing touch with the text.

Where there is a large chronological age difference between tutors and tutees, the readability of the material is likely to need controlling to a point below the tutor's level. However, avoid big ability differentials wherever possible. The tutor will certainly gain more and remain more interested if the reading ability differential is about 2 to 3 years. This is discussed further in the next subsection on Selection and matching.

While some books in school will already be graded for readability and pairs can thereby easily ensure that tutors are not overchallenged, once the pair begin to explore more widely the issue of readability of materials can become more problematic. Pairs should be taught a simple way of checking the readability of books. It should be made perfectly clear to them why they need to know and implement this.

One simple device is the 'finger' test. The tutor spreads 5 fingers on one hand and places them on 3 or 4 pages selected at random. If the tutor cannot read all 15 or 20 words touched by his or her fingertips, the book may well be too hard. As children become more used to choosing and to each other, they will develop their own more sophisticated methods, about which you can hold a class discussion.

In Paired Reading it is usual for the tutee to have a free choice of reading material. Sometimes, however, this can result in the tutor becoming bored, especially where tutor and tutee interests are very disparate. In this circumstance, it might be agreed that the tutor occasionally or alternately chooses the reading material.

When given free choice, many children develop or learn the skills of choosing appropriately within 2 or 3 weeks, and teachers should avoid interfering during the early period of a project in this respect. However, a small minority of children may still be all at sea about choosing appropriate books even after this time, and at this juncture teachers may need to step in to give a little gentle assistance and guidance, the aim being to develop choosing skills in the child rather than merely doing it for the child. Some very low ability children may need guidance from the outset, but this is rare.

As with parent tutoring, the sources for reading materials can be many and various, although some teachers experience initial difficulties in persuading children to leave the familiar security of the reading scheme. The number of books that the children get through will amaze you, and ideally they should be able to change their books on every occasion they are in contact. It may be logistically easier to mount a special additional collection in some convenient area.

Some children will wish to bring in books or magazines from home, and this should certainly be encouraged up to a point provided the readability level remains within the tutor's competence. Some children may begin bringing in comics, which may be accepted to some extent, but if it gets out of hand be prepared to impose a quota or ration on comic content.

Selection and matching of children

All teachers have experienced the great variations in general maturity level shown by classes in succeeding years. It would be particularly unwise to mount a project involving a large number of children where the maturity of many children to cope with the procedure is in grave doubt. In cases of uncertainty it is usually wisest to start a small pilot project with a few of the most mature children in the class acting as tutors, to enable further tutors to be added to the project subsequently as a 'privilege'.

Where the children have already been used to taking a degree of responsibility for independently guiding their own learning and/or working on cooperative projects in small groups, they may be expected to take to peer tutoring more readily. The gender balance in the class can represent a problem, particularly if there are more girls than boys, since some boys express extreme reluctance at the prospect of being tutored by a girl. Needless to say, this reluctance often disappears fairly quickly where the teacher allocates a female tutor to a male tutee and instructs them to get on with it, but the unfortunate tutee may still have great difficulty justifying what is going on to his friends in the playground.

The chronological age of the tutors and tutees needs considering separately. Do not assume that age and ability are synonymous. If you intend to use tutors who are considerably older than the tutees, unless you are fortunate enough to teach a vertically grouped class, you are likely to find the organization of the project considerably more complicated. This is especially true if the tutors are to be imported from another school. Same-age tutoring within one class is by far the easiest to organize.

Consideration of the overall number of pupils to be involved is also necessary. Start with a small number of children in the target group. Resist any temptation to include 'just one more', or before you know where you are the whole thing will become unmanageable. Particularly for a first venture, it is important to be able to closely monitor a small number of children. Do not worry about those who have to be 'excluded'. They can have a turn later, or be incorporated into the project as your organization becomes more fluent and automatic. If any evaluation is to be carried out, it will be useful to also check the progress of a comparison group of children who have not been involved in the peer tutoring.

The reading ability of the children is a critical factor in selection and matching of tutors and tutees. As we have said, as a general rule it is probably as well to keep a differential of about two years' reading age between tutors and tutees. Where same-age tutoring is to be established with a whole class, the children can be ranked in terms of scores on reading tests and a line drawn through the middle of the ranked list to separate tutors at the top from tutees at the bottom. Then the most able tutor is paired with the most able tutee, and so on. Other criteria for ranking could include reading scheme level or the teacher's observations/intuitive judgement.

However, the children's reading ability is by no means the only factor which must be taken into account. Pre-existing social relationships in the peer group must also be considered. To pair children with their 'best friends' of the moment might not be a good idea, particularly as the friendship may be of short duration. Obviously it would be undesirable to pair a child with another child with whom there is a pre-existing poor relationship. Another of the advantages of a same-age project is that one teacher is much more likely to know all the children involved, and thus can be more sensitive in taking social relationships into account.

It may or may not be desirable to take the individual preferences of the children themselves into account in some way. Some children may surprise you with the maturity they show in selecting a tutor they think would be effective in this role. However, to allow completely free child selection of tutor is likely to result in chaos. Some tutors would be overchosen; others not chosen at all, quite apart from the question of maintaining the requisite differential in reading ability.

One of the organizational difficulties with peer tutoring is the impact of absence from school of a tutor or tutee. It is always worthwhile to nominate a spare, stand-by or supply tutor or two, to ensure that absence from school of the usual tutor can be covered. Children acting as spare tutors need to be particularly stable, sociable and competent at reading, since they will have to work with a wide range of tutees. However, do not worry about imposing a burden on the spare tutors, as they may be expected to benefit the most in terms of increases in reading ability and self-esteem. The other obvious strategy for coping with absence is to attempt to rematch the children without partners, perhaps involving a change of role for some.

The question of parental agreement often arises in connection with peer tutor projects. Experience shows that involvement in such a project is usually sufficiently interesting for the children as to result in many of them mentioning it at home. This can result in some parents getting very strange ideas about what is going on. It is thus usually desirable for a brief note from school to be taken home by both tutors and tutees, explaining the project very simply. This should reassure parents that the project will have both academic and social benefits for tutors as well as tutees.

Organization of contact

A basic decision to be made is whether the tutoring is to occur wholly in class time, wholly in the children's break or recess time, or in a combination of both.

If the tutoring is to occur wholly in class time, it can be kept under teacher supervision. However, it will usually require timetabling, which may rob the exercise of a degree of desirable spontaneity. If the tutoring is to occur in the children's break time, more mature pairs can be left to make their own arrangements satisfactorily. This arrangement is a much greater imposition on tutors and tutees alike, however, and the momentum of the project may begin to peter out as the novelty begins to wear off. Some timetabling may thus be necessary even during the children's break time, so that the size and nature of the commitment involved is visible to all from the outset.

The best compromise is usually to schedule some minimum of contact for class time (perhaps three sessions per week), but allow the opportunity for pairs to do additional tutoring in their own break time if they so wish.

Finding the physical space to accommodate the pairs can be a problem. In a cross-age tutor project within a school, particularly where two full classes are involved, it is possible for half the pairs to work in the tutee's classroom and the other half in the tutor's classroom. Finding physical space for the tutoring to occur during break times may be considerably more difficult if there are problems of break-time supervision and/or children are not allowed access to classrooms.

Each individual tutoring period should last for a minimum of 15 minutes. Little worthwhile can occur in less time than this, after you have allowed for lack of punctuality and general settling down. If it is possible for the really enthusiastic to continue for over 20 or even 30 minutes, this is advantageous. It might be possible for the minimum 15 minutes to occur just before a natural break time but provide for the possibility of children continuing into their own break time if they so desire.

The frequency of tutorial contact should be three times each week as a basic minimum to ensure that the project has a significant and measurable impact. If peer tutoring occurs less frequently, it may have benefits, but they may not be measurable. If four or five contacts per week can be arranged, so much the better. Children involved in peer tutor projects rarely object to daily tutoring, as most of them find it interesting and rewarding. Some pairs may organize their own impromptu sessions in their own break times whether the teacher likes it or not!

The project should be launched with reference to an initial fixed period of commitment. It is useful for both tutors and tutees to be clear about what they are letting themselves in for, and how long a course they need to be able to sustain. A minimum project period of 6 weeks is suggested, since it will barely be possible to discern significant impact in less time than this. Popular project periods are 8 weeks and 10 weeks, which fit comfortably within an average term.

It is not usually desirable to fix a period of longer than 12 weeks for an initial commitment. It will be much better to review the project at the end of a short initial period, to evaluate the outcomes and make decisions about future directions jointly with the children, rather than letting the whole thing drift on interminably until it runs out of steam.

Training

It is neither effective nor ethically justifiable to turn the tutors loose on the unsuspecting tutees without giving them some form of training.

Just as with parent tutoring, before teachers set out to train children in particular procedures, it is important that the teachers themselves are well practised in the method to be used.

Sometimes the tutors and tutees are trained in two separate groups, but for Paired Reading it is best to train them together. As with parent training, the format of introduction, talk, demonstration, practice, feedback and coaching, questions, organizational details and written information should be followed.

The 'How To Do It' leaflet for parent tutoring (PRR1 in Chapter 2) will need some modification for peer tutoring. (It also needs some modification if being used in an adult literacy project, of course.) Changes will include: adding the rule about readability up to tutor's independent level, adding simple suggestion for checking readability, obvious modification to Time, Place and Notes sections, substitution of tutor for parent and tutee for child throughout.

Support and monitoring

During the course of the project, it is important that the coordinating teacher keeps a close eye on how things are going, in order to nip any incipient problems in the bud. In the spirit of cooperation which permeates peer tutoring, the children themselves may be the first to report difficulty or seek help. Such self-referral may revolve around asking the meaning of words which are unfamiliar to both tutor and tutee. Children also should be encouraged to readily report difficulties in accommodating to each other's habits without feeling that they are 'telling tales'.

Where a supervising teacher is present during the tutoring, much can be gleaned by observing individual pairs in rotation. The peer-tutoring session is not an opportunity for the teacher to 'get on with some marking'. On the contrary, the teacher either should be setting a good example by reading silently or with a tutee, or should be circulating round the group observing and guiding children as necessary. It is possible to ask a particularly expert child tutor (perhaps a stand-by tutor) who is not otherwise engaged to act as an observer in a similar way and report back to the teacher. The check list previously mentioned (PRR8 in Part Four Section A) will be useful for either teacher or peer monitor to help structure the observations. This check list can also be used as a self-assessment device by more mature pairs.

Some form of sessional self-recording during the project is probably desirable. It is a tangible demonstration of achievement for the children and of considerable interest for the supervising teacher. It is entirely logical that these records should be kept by the children themselves. Simple diaries similar to those suggested for parent projects (see PRR6 in Part Four Section A) can be kept by each pair. The tutee can record date and book read, while the tutor records some words of praise or other comment. The pair can refer to the Dictionary of Praise as necessary (see PRR7 in Part Four Section A).

Even quite young children acting as tutors can prove to be surprisingly good at writing positive comments about their tutees. Learning to give and receive praise without embarrassment is a valuable component of peer-tutor projects. The diaries are checked each week by the supervising teacher, who can also record some favourable comment and add an official signature if required.

In addition, it is often worthwhile calling occasional review meetings with tutors and tutees separately or together, in order to discuss in large or small groups how the project is going and what improvements could be made.

Feedback

A very simple way of presenting the favourable results and information to the children themselves is necessary to encourage them and promote further growth of confidence. A more 'scientific' collation will be necessary to present to interested colleagues. The information for this latter exercise need not necessarily be any less simple, merely different in emphasis.

At the end of the initial phase of the project, in the light of the evaluation and monitoring information, joint decisions have to be made about the future. At this point, the views of the children must be taken very much into account. Some may want to continue peer tutoring with the same frequency, others may wish to continue but with a lesser frequency, while a few may be wanting a complete rest, at least for a while.

When in doubt, a good rule of thumb is to go for the parsimonious option. It will be better to leave some of the children a little 'hungry', and have them pestering you to launch another project in six weeks time, rather than let peer tutoring meander on indefinitely until it quietly expires. At this point of decision-making also beware of trying to cater for a wide variety of choices from different tutoring pairs. The organisation of the project could become unbelievably complicated if you attempted to accommodate the varying desires for continuation of large numbers of children. It is probably as well to stick with what the majority vote for. Peer tutoring can thus be seen to be not only cooperative, but democratic as well.

Evaluation

As with parent tutoring, there is considerable virtue in building in some form of evaluation for the initial 'experimental' period of the project. This is especially true where the project is a first for the school.

The evaluation of Paired Reading projects is considered in detail in Chapter 5 – How To Evaluate Paired Reading.

CHAPTER 4

Does Paired Reading Work?

There has been a great deal of evaluative research on Paired Reading, particularly in the UK, North America, Australia and New Zealand. This could prove rather difficult to digest. A summary on reproducible masters for hand-outs or overhead projector transparencies, suitable for in-service training use, will be found in Part Four Section A (PRR 13).

This research will be reviewed in sub-sections:

> Pre–post (before and after) studies
> Control and comparison group studies
> Comparative studies (comparing Paired Reading with other methods)
> Reading process studies
> Reading style studies
> Follow-up studies
> Other features (miscellaneous)
> Summary of small-scale studies
> A large-scale field study
> Summary: comparison of small and large-scale studies
> Discussion and conclusions

Some of the subsections listed conclude with a summary. Those subsections titled 'Summary' will prove rather heavy going if you have not read anything else beforehand in this chapter.

The literature on Paired Reading is substantial. For the purposes of this review, papers that were descriptive and included no numerical outcome data were ignored. Studies relating to the use of Paired Reading in Further Education and Adult Literacy, studies of variations on the Paired Reading technique, and studies of Paired Reading with specialized groups such as children and adults with severe learning difficulties were all omitted, although relevant references for these special-ist areas will be found at the end of Part One of this book. Further studies will no doubt be discovered (e.g. Diaper (1989), Bamber (1990) and Atherley (1989)), but they are unlikely to significantly alter the conclusions below.

Throughout this chapter, 'Comprehension' scores refer to scores on separate comprehension scales for those tests featuring these (mainly the Neale Analysis of Reading Ability; Neale, 1966). Tests yielding only one score are all subsumed under the 'reading accuracy' category. Sometimes data reported were inadequate for the purposes of the current review. Statistical significance of findings was not always given or calculable. The quality of studies was extremely varied.

The studies reviewed incorporated various 'intensive periods' of participation, and furthermore almost all gave reading test results in terms of 'reading ages' rather than standardized deviation scores or quotients. In order to enable some approxim-ate comparison of studies incorporating different lengths of intensive period, reference will be made to rates of gain or 'ratio gains'. Ratio gain can be defined as the gain in reading age made by a subject on a reading test during a chronological time span, expressed as a ratio of that time span. That is, ratio gain equals reading age gain in months divided by chronological time span in months.

Ratio gains are sometimes construed as a multiple of 'normal' rates of gain in reading, on the assumption that a 'normal' gain is one month of reading age per chronological month elapsed. This fallacious assumption ignores the non-linearity of reading development and the non-equivalence of one month of reading age gain from differing reading age baselines. The validity of the use of ratio gains is extremely doubtful, and some readers may prefer to focus on raw gains. This latter approach does, however, render the highly heterogeneous literature very difficult to summarize.

Pre-Post Studies

Eighteen pre-post studies are reported by Barrett (1986), Bush (1983, 1985), Bushell *et al.* (1982), Byron (1987), Crombie and Low (1986), Evans (1984), Gollop (1984), Kidd and Levey (1983), McMillan *et al.* (1988), Morgan (1976), Morgan and Lyon (1979), Pitchford and Taylor (1983), Sweetlove (1985) and Winter (1985, 1987). They are very varied in participant age (6–13 years), participant group size (2–65), project length (4–18 weeks) and outcomes (ratio gains from 1.26 to 8.67 in reading accuracy and from 0.73 to 9.08 in comprehension).

Fifteen deployed natural parents, two peer tutors and one parent volunteers in school. Eight different reading tests were used for evaluation, predominantly the Neale Analysis (in thirteen cases). One study focused on dyslexic children and another on children in a special school for moderate learning difficulties. In one ten-week project the first five weeks were wholly preoccupied with Reading Together.

Control and Comparison Group Studies

Control group studies are generally considered by researchers to yield better quality data capable of supporting firmer conclusions. However, the quality of studies varies even within this category. Weaker studies might have flaws such as: small size of experimental or control group, doubtful comparability of control and experimental groups irrespective of method of allocation to groups, impurity of Paired Reading technique as trained, and other atypical factors in project organization such as poor monitoring, infrequent tutoring, over-control of reading materials and unusually short or long project periods. Compensating research design strengths include blind testing and equivalent extra reading practice for control groups.

On this basis, the eighteen control or comparison group studies can be divided into bands of different quality, low (5) to high (1). Band 5 includes Gautrey (1988), Jungnitz, Olive and Topping (1983), Low and Davies (1988), Richardson (1986) and Spalding *et al.* (1984). Band 4 includes Bush (1982), Lees (1986), Limbrick *et al.* (1985) and Morgan and Gavin (1988). Band 3 includes Byron and Brock (1984), Grundy (1987), O'Hara (1985) and Simpson (1985). Band 2 includes Heath (1981) and Low *et al.* (1987). Band 1 includes Carrick-Smith (1982), Crombie and Low (1986) and Miller *et al.* (1986).

These studies are also very varied in participant age (5–13 years), participant and control group size (3–33), project length (4–39 weeks) and outcomes (ratio gains for participants from 0.94 to 9.75 in reading accuracy and from 0.96 to 9.27 in comprehension; for controls from −0.43 to 4.88 in accuracy and from −0.13 to 7.11 in comprehension).

Twelve deployed natural parents, six peer tutors and two parent volunteers in school (some had more than one tutor type). Seven different reading tests were used for evaluation, predominantly the Neale Analysis (in twelve cases). Further summary details will be found in Topping and Lindsay (1992c).

Comparative Studies

The twenty-two studies comparing Paired Reading to some other method can also be placed in quality bands. Band 5 (low quality) includes: Loveday and Simmons (1988), Spiby (1986), Sweetlove (1987) and Winter (1988). Band 4 includes: Heath (1981), Jungnitz (1984), Wareing (1983) and Winter (1985). Band 3 includes: Burdett (1985), Grigg (1984), Jones (1987) and Thirkell (1989). Bands 2/1 combined include: Dening (1985), Joscelyne (1989, 1991), Leach and Siddal (1990), Lindsay *et al.* (1985) and Welch (1985).

These studies are also very varied in participant age (5–12 years), participant and alternative treatment group size (4–30 and 4–45 respectively), project length (5–26 weeks) and outcomes (ratio gains for participants from 0.28 to 8.32 in reading accuracy and from 0.96 to 10.18 in comprehension; for alternative treatments from −0.18 to 7.30 in accuracy and from 0.05 to 9.77 in comprehension). Some of these studies also had control groups.

Twelve deployed natural parents, nine peer tutors and three parent volunteers in school (some had more than one tutor type). Six different reading tests were used for evaluation, predominantly the Neale Analysis (in seventeen cases). Alternative treatments included: Listening, Listening and Prompting, Listening and Praising, Listening and Error Correction, Listening and Retelling, Pause Prompt Praise, Silent Reading, Reading Together, 'Relaxed Reading' and Corrective Reading with and without Paired Reading. Further summary details will be found in Topping and Lindsay (1992c).

Process Studies

Relatively few studies of Paired Reading have reported detailed information on the behaviour of participants subsequent to training during involvement in projects. It cannot be assumed that participants' behaviour was standard throughout, i.e. that training actually works, especially in the longer term.

Morgan and Lyon (1979) collected detailed baseline and post-training data on the percentage of words read that were verbally reinforced by parent tutors. In the four participating pairs, percentage of words verbally reinforced rose from 0 during baseline to between 50 and 75 per cent for participants subsequent to training, which took place on a one-to-one basis during several lengthy sessions amounting to between 3 and 45 hours in total.

Bushell *et al.* (1992) in Derbyshire completed observational check lists relating to parent and child behaviour while observing pairs in action during follow-up home visits (this is reported in more detail in Miller 1987). Observational check lists on elements of the Paired Reading technique covered Reading Together (synchrony, parental adjustment of pace, child attention to each word, parent allowing time for self-correction, parent remodelling errors) and Reading Alone (child signals, parent responds, child praised, parent indicates minor errors, return to Reading Together after 4 seconds, child praised regularly). The researchers also checked whether reading material was chosen by the child and whether parents avoided negative and anxiety-provoking comments. Check lists were completed subjectively and no data on inter-rater reliability are given. Check lists completed were grouped into overall 'high' and 'low' quality of Reading Together and Reading Alone.

For Reading Together, forty-four check lists were rated as high quality and ten as low quality. Widespread difficulty was indicated with parental praise for signalling and for independent reading, so the praise item was ignored in adjudicating 'quality'. For Reading Alone, thirty-seven check lists were judged high quality and seventeen low quality. However, comparison on specific check-list items between the high and low-quality groups indicated differences reaching statistical significance in only one case (return to Reading Together after 4 seconds during Reading Alone).

Only four aspects of the process of use of the Paired Reading technique studied correlated with reading accuracy gains on reading tests: quality of independent reading ($+0.27$), percentage of words read independently ($+0.25$), the quality of simultaneous reading ($+0.10$), and the total time spent on Paired Reading (less than 0.10). Statistical significance of coefficients is not given, but the last two are unlikely to be educationally significant. The Derbyshire workers were surprised by these results, as they had thought Reading Together would be the more important aspect of the process, and they speculated that Reading Together was important in the elimination of parental criticism, thereby having an impact on all aspects of subsequent parental behaviour.

A more detailed study of ten participants in the Derbyshire project was conducted by Toepritz (1982), who audio-taped three follow-up home visits for each participant. The tapes were then analysed with respect to the Derbyshire 'Check List of Elements of Paired Reading', and an inter-rater reliability of 73 per cent is cited. Over the time span covered by the three consecutive home visits, the percentage of time spent on independent reading with pairs rose, but this was not found to be related to reading age gains to a statistically significant degree. The quality of Reading Together was found to be very varied, but this did not appear to be related to reading age gains either. No correlations achieved statistical significance, largely a function of the small number of children in the study, the largest correlation of 0.44 being between time spent in independent reading and reading accuracy gains.

Elliott (1989) conducted *post hoc* interviews with parents who had participated in Paired Reading projects and made audio-recordings of some families, in a pilot project including nine interviewed subjects and a main project in a different school including thirteen interviewed subjects. The participating children were mixed ability 6–7-year-olds. In the main study, fifteen of thirty parents had been 'listening' to their children read before the Paired Reading project.

After training, seventeen of the thirty parents did not use the Paired Reading technique 'perfectly'. Two pairs did only Reading Together, two only Reading Alone, three had difficulties Reading Together and six tended to switch from Paired Reading to 'listening' as they went along. In four cases pairs did not continue because the child rejected the technique and in two cases because the parents rejected the technique. As time went on, there tended to be more reversion to 'informal listening'.

Elliot concluded that in many cases the Paired Reading technique was integrated with a pre-existing method. However, the interview data support the view that Paired Reading results in reduction of stress in the reading relationship and the error correction procedure does result in the retention of sight vocabulary. It should be noted that the degree of conformity to 'pure' technique was much greater for participants in the pilot scheme.

Turning to process studies of peer-tutored Paired Reading, Limbrick *et al.* (1985) collected very detailed process data on three pairs, in which tutors were aged 10–11 years and tutees 6–8 years, using a minor modification of the Paired Reading technique. Pretraining baseline measures and post-training measures were made of: amount of discussion, praise for correct responses, praise for independent reading, attention to errors, supplying of unknown words, eliciting positive responses and avoiding negative comments.

Each pair was observed weekly, but no data on inter-rater reliability are given. Post-training, substantial increases in praise for both correct responding and independent reading were evident, together with increases in prompting to elicit the correct response from the tutee. Amount of attention to error showed some small increase, but amount of supplying unknown words and amount of negative comments stayed much the same.

Winter (1988) conducted a process analysis based on audio-recordings with eighteen pupils participating in projects in two schools, However, a disproportionate number of subjects was included from one school, which showed substantially poorer outcome results on reading tests, and the selection of subjects for process data collection was far from random. Inter-rater reliabilities ranged from 0.28 to 0.93, some of these being unacceptably low. Measures were taken of the number of errors corrected, the numbers of errors uncorrected and the amount of positive verbal reinforcement. Attempts were made to collect data with reference to other measures but it proved impossible to do this reliably.

Winter reports that the mean use of praise was less than 1 in 200 words (less than twice in 5 minutes), and 6 pairs used none at all. It was also reported that uncorrected errors outweighed corrected errors in a ration of 4:1. Pairs were, however, uniformly conscientious about using modelling for error correction and this method accounted for 98 per cent of the error correction observed. Considerable consistency of participant behaviour across observational sessions was reported, and it was noted that correlations between process measures and reading age gains failed to reach statistical significance.

Joscelyne (1989) notes that in her peer-tutored Paired Reading projects there was a tendency for 'pairs (to) drift into other methods of reading'. Close monitoring was necessary to ensure adherence to the Paired Reading technique.

Summary

In both the parent-tutored and peer-tutored process data, many contradictory findings are evident. It is obviously possible for participants to manifest the required process behaviour but this would appear to be more likely in studies of smaller numbers of participants, especially when the training has been more detailed. In larger studies of parent-tutored Paired Reading, conformity to good technique has been found in from 75 to 43 per cent of participants, the higher figure being associated with home visits. Given the paucity of process research, the relation between process and outcome remains obscure. The vast majority of studies have evaluated on a crude input–output model. Therefore, output variables may reflect more the structure of service delivery (training and follow-up) than the impact of a particular technique that is assumed to have been applied.

Reading Style Studies

A number of studies using the Neale Analysis have measured changes in rate of reading on the test passages on a pre–post basis. In some of these studies (for example, Lindsay and Evans, 1985) a reduction in the rate of reading at post-test after Paired Reading was found, although in other studies (for example, Winter 1985) an increase in rate of reading is reported (of 17 per cent in this case). Measuring of rate of reading using the Neale Analysis has thus yielded various results. Other researchers have measured rate of reading on samples of text specifically selected for the purpose from a variety of sources, and results from these studies will be referred to in greater detail below.

Most reading style studies have applied some form of miscue or error analysis on a pre–post basis, using parallel but different texts of similar readability on the two occasions. Four studies report data for reading style change from parent-tutored projects.

Bush (1982) applied the miscue analysis structure proposed in the Neale Analysis to seven participant and eighteen comparison children aged 9–11 who were at least one year retarded in reading. Miscues of the control group showed little change from pre- to post-test. The miscues of the participant Paired Reading group showed a reduction in refusals from 58 to 31 per cent and an increase of 19 per cent in substitutions. Paired Readers also showed substantial increases on the Daniels and Diack Tests of phonic skills, but the difference between participant and control children did not reach statistical significance. Differences between participant and control groups on tests of visual and auditory sequential memory likewise showed no statistically significant differences.

Four participants in the Derbyshire project were investigated in detail by Scott (1983), who used pre- and post-measures on the Aston Index (Newton *et al.*, 1979) together with a miscue analysis on a set passage. Only one subject showed any improvement on the Aston Subtests, and his gain in reading age was minimal. The miscue analysis showed an increased tendency among the Paired Readers towards the use of contextual cues, although this was not regular or predictable.

Winter (1985) collected reading style data on ten of thirty-three subjects involved in a project, all of whom were below-average readers aged 9–11 years. The ten subjects were audio-taped reading a text of controlled readability on a pre- and post-test basis. In this study, parents were trained in both Paired Reading and Pause, Prompt, Praise. At post-test, rate of reading on a similar text had increased, errors as a percentage of words read decreased by 22 per cent, refusals decreased by 28 per cent and the proportion of self-corrections remained the same.

There were no significant differences in changes in reading style between parents reporting using Paired Reading and those reporting using Praise, Prompt, Praise.

Similar methodology was used by Green (1987) on eighteen of forty-four children involved in a four-week summer programme for the children of migrant farm workers in the United States, not all of whom were actually doing Paired Reading as prescribed. Only one reading style indicator was checked, namely, the semantic appropriateness of miscues. In thirteen out of eighteen cases improvements in this area were evident. Of these thirteen, ten were definitely doing Paired Reading. However, the mean increase was modest (9 per cent).

Eight studies have concerned themselves with changes in reading style in peer-tutored Paired Reading projects. The first of these was that of Winter and Low (1984), who reported data only on their fifteen ten- to eleven-year-old tutees, in a same-age peer-tutored project based in one class. Different texts of similar readability were applied on a pre- and post-participation basis and students were tape-recorded reading them. The tutees' rate of reading rose by an average of 30 per cent, error rate fell by an average of 50 per cent, percentage of self-correction as a proportion of all errors rose by 70 per cent, and percentage of refusals as a proportion of all errors fell from 7 per cent to zero. On the whole, these changes were less marked for the most retarded tutees, except that for these the percentage of refusals dropped even more sharply.

A project which incorporated follow-up data in which 11–12-year-old remedial pupils in a high school were tutored by 16–18-year-old students is reported by Cawood and Lee (1985) and Lee (1986). Of twenty-two participant tutees, data for reading style change are reported for 16, the same two passages of controlled readability being used on both occasions. For all sixteen the percentage of errors fell, for twelve of the sixteen the percentage of refusals reduced and for twelve of the sixteen the percentage of errors that were self-corrected improved. Ten tutees showed an increase in speed of reading in words per minute while four stayed the same and two became slower.

Follow-up data one year later were gathered on thirteen tutees, dropping the easier of the two original texts and adding a new one of much higher readability. Over the year since pre-test, the percentage of errors had reduced by 41 per cent on average overall, the percentage of self-corrections had increased by 135 per cent and the percentage of errors that were contextually relevant had increased by 100 per cent. Lee concluded that there was evidence that changes in reading style accruing from a brief cross-age peer–tutor project showed no signs of wash-out at long-term follow-up, even though no tutoring had occurred in the interim.

Limbrick *et al.* (1985) deployed three tutors aged 10–11 years with three tutees aged 6–8 years, all of whom were retarded in reading. The tutors and tutees read graded passages taken from classroom reading materials and answered comprehension questions based upon them. Two tape recordings were made weekly and measures of reading accuracy and proportion of self-corrections taken from them. In addition, Cloze comprehension exercises were completed weekly by participants, and the syntactic and semantic appropriateness of Clozes was assessed. During the participant period, there was evidence of a rapid rise in reading accuracy and self-correction, a rapid recovery from the impact of change to more difficult materials being apparent. The proportion of appropriate substitutions rose and the proportion of correct responses to comprehension questions did likewise. This was true for both tutors and tutees.

Results contrary to the general tendencies evident in other studies were reported by Lees (1986, 1987). Ten Paired Readers aged 10–12 years who were on average 2.8 years retarded in reading were compared on repeated subskill tests to a similar non-participant group and to a non-participant group of 8–9-year-old average readers. Assessment was made of word pronunciation, non-word pronunciation, semantic appropriateness, lexical appropriateness, visual matching, phonological segmentation and use of context. Although the Paired Reading group showed the largest increase in reading age, there was no evidence of an increase in the use of context by this group. In fact, there was some evidence to suggest an improvement in decoding skills, by 'phonic or direct visual access'. The non-participant group of elderly, retarded readers was found at pre-test to use context as much as the younger, average readers.

Low *et al.* (1987) used seven graded reading passages covering a wide range of readability with their thirteen tutorial pairs and twenty-six control children. The error rate of the tutors fell by 71 per cent compared to a control group reduction of 59 per cent. The error rate of the tutees fell by 50 per cent compared to a control group reduction of 42 per cent. The participant group changes were more pronounced for girls than for boys.

Two studies are reported by Joscelyne (1989), the second being a replication of the first, both comparing a group of Paired Readers with another group where the tutors merely 'listened'. In the first study, both groups showed a small reduction in the number of errors. The Paired Reading group showed a 15 per cent increase in the proportion of errors that were substitutions, while the listening group showed no change, and this difference was statistically significant. The Paired Reading group showed a reduction of 6 per cent in refusals while the listening group showed an increase of 5 per cent, and this difference reached statistical significance. There were no statistically significant differences between the two groups on the proportion of substitutions that were grapho-phonemically or contextually appropriate. Likewise, on a phonics test, the number of errors fell for both groups but the difference between them was not statistically significant.

In the replication with eleven Paired Reading pairs and a similar number of listening pairs, two passages matched for readability were used, and tutees were tested on key words appearing in the passages, first in isolation and subsequently in context. The difference between words read in isolation correctly and words read in context correctly was calculated for both groups, to constitute an index of change in the use of contextual information. The Paired Readers showed an increase in the extent to which they read more words correctly in context than in isolation, but this was not true of the listening groups, and this difference reached statistical significance.

However, later studies by Joscelyne (1991) yielded more contradictory findings with respect to changes in the reading style of peer tutees. In one experiment, Paired

Readers showed reduced error rates but so did a reading aloud group. Substitution rates increased and refusal rates decreased for Paired Readers more than those reading aloud, but differences were not large, perhaps owing to ceiling effects on the tests employed. In a further two experiments, error rates decreased in Paired Readers but refusal rates showed some minor increase. In one case substitution rates increased while in the other they decreased. However, in the last of these studies, Paired Readers did show improved use of context. Joscelyne's complex and sometimes contradictory data merit closer scrutiny.

One study has considered changes in reading style as a result of Paired Reading tutoring by teachers (Welch, 1985), and here again a listening group was compared to a Paired Reading group. Measures were taken of the use of context, comprehension, rate of reading and number of refusals. The Paired Reading group did better on all measures than the listening group, but none of the differences reached statistical significance.

Summary

Considering parent, peer and teacher-tutored studies together, in eight of these studies error rates have been found to reduce in Paired Readers and in no cases have error rates increased. In seven cases, Paired Readers showed decreases in refusal rates and in two cases an increase. In seven cases, use of context showed an increase, in one case no difference was found, and in no case was there a decrease. In four cases the rate or speed of reading showed an increase and in no case was there a decrease (but it should be noted that studies using the Neale Analysis as a measure of rate of reading have yielded increases and decreases). In four studies, self-correction rate showed an increase and in no case a decrease. In three cases the use of phonics showed an increase and in no case was there a decrease. Although many of the differences cited did not reach statistical significance and only a few studies used either control or comparison groups who were non-participant or used another technique, strong consistent trends emerge from all these studies considered together.

The general pattern is of Paired Reading resulting in fewer refusals (greater confidence), greater fluency, greater use of the context and a greater likelihood of self-correction, as well as fewer errors (greater accuracy) and better phonic skills.

Follow-up Studies

Follow-up data gathered some time after the end of the intensive period of projects have been reported in five studies in the literature, two wholly parent tutored, one cross-age peer tutored, one deploying a combination of natural parent, cross-age peer and adult volunteer tutors, and one incorporating tutoring by professionals.

Bushell et al. (1982) reported six-month follow-up data on an unspecified number of subjects in the pilot Derbyshire study. Considerable differences were evident between three different participating schools. For reading accuracy on the Neale Analysis, the children from two schools appeared to reach a plateau after the intensive period, while in a third school the participants continued to improve their reading test scores at the same accelerated rate as was evident during the intensive period. In reading comprehension on the Neale Analysis, subjects at one school had regressed on average at follow-up, although not back to the pre-test level. Subjects at a second school maintained progress at normal rates (that is, their gains from the intensive period showed no sign of wash-out). A third group maintained accelerated progress at less than the pre-post rate but at a greater than normal rate. It was not known if families continued to do Paired Reading after the end of the intensive period – they were certainly not given any specific encouragement to continue.

Bushell concludes that, with respect to follow-up gains, the 'nature of school involvement is an important factor'.

A study of just five 10-year-old weak readers by Lees (1985) also used the Neale Analysis at follow-up 13 weeks after the end of the intensive period. However, in this case the initial intensive period involved tutoring by a teacher, while during the 13-week follow-up period parents were trained to continue with Paired Reading for a minimum of five sessions per week. During the intensive 10-week period of teacher tutoring on a twice-weekly basis, participants made average ratio gains of 3.2 in reading accuracy and 1.3 in reading comprehension. During the subsequent 13 weeks of parental tutoring, the subjects made mean ratio gains of 2.6 in accuracy and 2.1 in comprehension. Albeit with small numbers, this study thus demonstrated that continuing gains were possible with continuing input.

A longer-term follow-up, 46 weeks after post-test and a full year after pre-test, was reported by Carrick-Smith (1982). This project involved pupils from three high schools who at pre-test were 11–12 years old and up to 3 years retarded in reading. Tutoring was variously by parents, cross-age peer tutors and adult volunteers. Separate follow-up results are not given for the three tutor groups, and the composite follow-up sample was twenty-seven subjects. On Neale Analysis accuracy, over the 10.6 month follow-up period, participant children made further mean gains of 8.1 months of reading age while controls gained 6.6 months. In comprehension, mean participant gain was 10.2 months and mean control gain 6.8 months.

Thus gains in both accuracy and comprehension for participant subjects were greater than for control or comparison subjects, but even participant gains during the follow-up period were less than 'normal'. However, there was great variance between subjects and between schools in the follow-up data, in both reading accuracy and reading comprehension. As with the Bushell (1982) study, one school contributed disproportionately to the experimental gains at follow-up.

Lee (1986) reported 12-month follow-up data on thirteen of twenty-two participants in a cross-age peer tutored Paired Reading project in which the tutees were high-school 'remedial' pupils aged 11–13 years. On the Daniels and Diack Test 12, the participant tutees gained 1.2 years of reading age during the pre–post participant period and a further 0.5 years during the post-test to follow-up period. The control subjects gained 0.7 years from pre- to post-test and only a further 0.2 years during the follow-up period. Total gains from pre-test to follow-up test for participants were thus 1.7 years of reading age on average, and only 0.9 years for control children.

As in the Carrick-Smith (1982) study, gains during the follow-up period were less for both groups than would normally be expected, although the differential favouring the participant group remained. Lee also reported follow-up data for participant tutees on changes in reading style, based on error analysis of oral reading of passages of variously controlled readability. As noted in the previous section on reading style, over the whole pre-test to follow-up period, errors fell by 41 per cent, self-corrections increased by 135 per cent and contextual appropriate errors increased by 100 per cent. Lee concluded that the changes in reading style among the participants evident at post-test endured and were consolidated through to follow-up a year later, even though no further tutoring had occurred in the interim.

Burdett (1985) gathered follow-up data just 4 weeks after the end of the intensive period, in a study in which children aged 8–11 years who were approximately 1 year retarded in reading were tutored by professionals. The Widespan Reading Test and an analysis of error rate were the outcome measures. Subsamples of children also experienced Paired Reading at home with natural parents, while others did not. Burdett found that both experimental groups (parents involved and not involved) had retained highly significant gains over control groups, whether using the Paired Reading technique or the 'individualized reading' approach based on Pause, Prompt and Praise.

On average, experimental subjects made three times more progress than controls. The error rate of the Paired Reading group at follow-up had shown a further decrease by 25 per cent, while the individualized reading group showed a further decrease of 11 per cent, compared to an increase in the control group of 9 per cent. Concerning reading style, Burdett reported that the diagnostic indicators in the Widespan Test suggested that Paired Reading resulted in improvements in both decoding and psycholinguistic capabilities, while the individualized approach resulted in increases in decoding skills only. The additional benefit of parental involvement became increasingly apparent at follow-up testing.

Summary

Even within the same study, follow-up gains may vary considerably from school to school. Continued acceleration at above 'normal' rates is relatively rare, and indeed some follow-up gains cited are less than normal rates, while still remaining better than those of control or comparison groups. Follow-up periods have varied greatly, ranging from 4 weeks to 12 months, but the length of follow-up does not appear to relate consistently to the favourability of follow-up findings.

The standard of the studies is not high. However, there is relatively little suggestion here of wash-out of experimental gains, this being reported for only a small number of subjects in one school in one study. ('Wash-out' is defined here as a decline in rate of acceleration to below pre-project levels, resulting in overall 'normal' progress or less over the total period from baseline to follow-up testing. It is considered unrealistic to expect acceleration at above normal rates to continue indefinitely. Thus, the term 'wash-out' is used here to refer to erosion of relative gain, not of relative acceleration, at follow-up.)

There is evidence that acceleration can be sustained and even increased with the deployment of different types of tutor consecutively, and that changes in reading style can also endure in the long term.

Other Features

A small number of studies incorporate an attempt to measure changes in self-concept by means of a paper-and-pencil instrument, but results have been extremely erratic and sometimes wholly implausible (for example, Carrick-Smith 1982).

A larger number of studies incorporate some information about client satisfaction as indicated by recorded verbal responses or questionnaire completion. Unfortunately, the many different formats in which this feedback is expressed render it impossible to summarize. However, Topping and Whiteley (1990) reported a large-scale study of this type using the same measures throughout.

If children 'learn to read by reading', one factor in the effectiveness of Paired Reading (or any supplemental tutoring scheme) might be expected to be the influence of extra reading practice alone. Thus, other things being equal, more time spent doing Paired Reading should be associated with greater gains in reading skill. Some workers have explored this relationship. Bushell *et al.* (1982) reported very small correlation coefficients between reading accuracy and comprehension and time spent reading during a Paired Reading project (accuracy 0.15, comprehension 0.33; n=19). This finding was repeated in their later and larger controlled study (accuracy 0.008, comprehension 0.142; Miller *et al.* 1986).

Carrick-Smith (1982), Wareing (1983) and Dening (1985) likewise found no statistically significant correlation between total time spent doing Paired Reading and test gains. Dening did, however, report a positive correlation (0.43) between frequency of tutoring and gains made, which was also true of her comparison Pause, Prompt, Praise group but not the Listening group. By contrast, Morgan and Gavin (1988) found no such significant relationship. However, few of these studies used very adequate measures of 'time on task', tending to rely on participant self-recording.

A few studies have included other measures in the attempt to demonstrate peripheral benefits from Paired Reading. One was that of Jungnitz *et al.* (1983), who noted increased scores on the English Picture Vocabulary Test when 21 non-reading 7-year-olds were involved in Paired Reading over a long period. The mean standardized score rose from 95.9 to 99.98 (in a highly disadvantaged area), the difference attaining statistical significance. Evans (1984) similarly noted large gains on the British Picture Vocabulary Scale for 6 'dyslexic' high-school subjects.

Some workers have used Paired Reading in combination with other approaches in the context of an intervention, and then been unable to demonstrate which aspect(s) of the project resulted in which elements of overall gains made. An example is the work of Young and Tyre (1983), who deployed a number of variations on Paired Reading sequentially and/or simultaneously according to the needs of individual participants, together with parent-tutored writing and spelling activities and a 'holiday school'. Over 1 year, the control group advanced 0.8 years on a reading test, while a 'dyslexic' experimental group advanced 1.8 years and a 'remedial' experimental group 2.0 years.

Cooknell (1985) involved parents in workshops where they were taught a simple 'listening' method, Pause, Prompt and Praise and Paired Reading, as well as a more complex 'linguistic' approach focusing on comprehension. Cooknell notes 'it could be that we asked too much of the parents' and gains on reading tests were modest. Ripon *et al.* (1986) combined the Reading Together aspect of Paired Reading with Datapac Reading, a precision teaching approach. Baseline, pre-post and follow-up data from the Spar and BAS reading tests showed marked acceleration from baseline during the project period. This was sustained at short-term follow-up for three out of four data sets.

Holdsworth (1985, 1986) reported on workshops based in a special school for children with learning difficulties, in which parents were taught Reading Together, precision teaching and direct instruction (DISTAR) approaches to mesh with the curriculum of the school as experienced by their children. A mean ratio gain of 2.0 over a long period of intervention is cited, but it is uncertain to what this improvement can be attributed. Sweetlove's (1987) comparative study suggested that direct instruction alone (Corrective Reading) was less effective in raising reading accuracy than Paired Reading alone, and that the combination of the two yielded only a small incremental gain over Paired Reading alone. However, Sweetlove's experimental groups were not equivalent.

Also of interest are attempts to apply Paired Reading to 'special' populations. These have included its deployment with pupils in special schools for children with moderate learning difficulties, severe learning difficulties and behavioural difficulties. Relevant references include Booth and Winter (1987); Dickinson (1986, 1987); Green (1987); Holdsworth (1985, 1986); Jones (1988); Jungnitz *et al.* (1983); McKnight (1985); O'Hara (1985a, 1985b, 1986); Scoble *et al.* (1988); Scoble (1989); Topping (1986b); Topping and McKnight (1984); Topping *et al.* (1985); Tyre and Young (1985); Ulmer and Green (1988); and Young and Tyre (1983).

Reports on the use of Paired Reading with families of South Asian origin, often where parental skills in speaking and reading English are limited, have been provided by Jungnitz (1984, 1985), Bush (1985), Welsh and Roffe (1985), Vaughey and MacDonald (1986) and Topping (1992a). A training video demonstrating Paired Reading on single and dual-language texts in English, Urdu and Gujerati has been produced (Topping and Shaikh 1989).

Bush (1985) reports interesting data on relative take-up rates from ethnic groups in a multi-ethnic school. Highest take-up was from Afro-Caribbean families and lowest from white families, with Asian families involving themselves just a little more (proportionately) than whites. Among the reports of usage of Paired Reading in the United States is one by Ulmer and Green (1988). They trained parents who were migrant summer farm-workers in rural areas of Vermont to use the technique with their children while supported by peripatetic teachers during a (moving) 'summer school'. No numerical data were cited, but this population was found challenging in terms of service delivery.

Summary of Small-Scale Studies

In 20 pre-post design parent-tutored projects incorporating 333 Paired Readers, mean ratio gains in accuracy were 5.19 and in comprehension 6.82. In 13 parent-tutored control group projects incorporating 212 Paired Readers, ratio gains were considerably lower at 3.13 for accuracy and 3.91 for comprehension. In 12 parent-tutored projects comparing different techniques incorporating 141 Paired Readers, mean ratio gains for accuracy were 3.24 and for comprehension 4.08, very similar to those for Paired Readers in control group studies.

The overall mean pre-post ratio gain for the 686 Paired Readers involved in all types of small-scale parent-tutored study was 4.15 for accuracy and 5.33 for comprehension, when the ratio gains in each study were weighted by the number of subjects in each study. The pattern of lower mean pre-post ratio gains in control and comparative parent-tutored studies than in simple pre-post studies is not repeated in the data for peer–tutor projects.

Mean pre–post ratio gains of Paired Reading peer tutees are very similar in reading accuracy irrespective of the type of study, averaging 4.77 overall for 12 projects incorporating 291 Paired Readers. For tutee comprehension the mean ratio gain is 6.14, but this is based on only 87 subjects. Considering mean pre-post ratio gains of Paired Readers in all types of study together, it is evident that on average outcomes in both reading accuracy and reading comprehension are as good for participants tutored by peers as those tutored by parents. Indeed, the tutee results from peer–tutor projects are somewhat better.

The outcomes for the peer tutors themselves are on average similar to those for the tutees, albeit slightly less good, although these results are depressed by disproportionate representation from one particular research venue.

Overall, mean pre-post ratio gains for all 60 projects yielding norm-referenced data were 4.23 for accuracy (n=1012) and 5.37 for comprehension (n=703) including outcomes for peer tutors and tutees.

Considering parent-tutored control group studies specifically, mean pre–post ratio gain in accuracy for Paired Readers was 3.13 (n=212) while that for control subjects was 1.19 (n=195). In comprehension, mean ratio gain for participants was 3.91 and for controls 1.93. The latter figure demonstrates the need for caution in interpreting scores in comprehension on the Neale Analysis. For peer tutees in six projects, mean participant ratio gains in accuracy were 5.34 (n=57) and for controls 1.48 (n=56). Peer tutors demonstrated a mean ratio gain in accuracy of 5.90 (n=51) while their controls were markedly lower at 3.63, although still substantially above 'normal' rates of gain. There was a similar pattern for peer–tutor reading comprehension, but sample numbers were again very small.

Overall, in 19 control group studies, mean experimental accuracy ratio gain was 3.97 (n=320), the equivalent control figure being 1.57 (n=290). In comprehension, mean experimental ratio gain was 4.87 (n=206) and control ratio gain 2.30 (n=192).

Results from studies including control groups can also be aggregated using meta-analytic techniques which generate effect size indicators. Various kinds of effect size indicator are in use. For the purposes of this review Glass's delta (Glass *et al.* 1981) will be used. This is one of the longer established indices of this type. Glass's delta standardizes the mean gain of the experimental group by subtracting from it the mean gain of the control group and dividing by the standard deviation of the control group. It is thus impossible to compute if the standard deviation of the control group gains is not given.

Seven out of nineteen studies incorporating control groups did not include information about variance in control group gain. The mean effect size for parent tutees was 1.57 for accuracy and 1.41 for comprehension, the latter showing considerably more variability. These indicators are drawn from eight projects of which seven had comprehension data, incorporating 142 Paired Readers. The effect sizes for peer tutees and peer tutors are drawn from a much smaller number of projects involving a much smaller number of subjects.

Peer tutees show a very large effect size (4.44) for reading accuracy, but with very great variability. In these 12 control group projects, the overall effect size for reading accuracy was 2.12 and that for reading comprehension 1.63, irrespective of nature of tutor and including results from peer tutors and tutees. How meaningful this is, given the great variability in effect sizes, is debatable. However, the effect sizes evident here are large when compared to those cited in other meta-analytic reports (for example, Cohen *et al.* 1982).

Overall, in the 12 control group projects for which requisite data were available, mean effect size for reading accuracy was 2.12 (n=218) and 1.63 for comprehension (n=164), (median 1.40 and 1.14, respectively).

Of 22 studies comparing Paired Reading to other techniques, in 18 cases statistical significance of findings is given, and in seven of these Paired Reading significantly out-performed other techniques (almost always reading aloud/listening, in 5 out of 7 cases with peer tutors). A number of other studies found Paired Reading superior but the difference did not attain statistical significance in small samples, and two studies found significant differences in other measures of reading skill. No study found Paired Reading significantly inferior. In many studies, sample size was so small that finding statistical significance was unlikely.

However, in the 15 studies yielding adequate, norm-referenced data, the mean pre-post ratio gain in accuracy for Paired Readers was 3.9 and that for other techniques 2.7 (peer–tutor results included). Some studies report contamination between groups supposedly using different techniques, but some process studies have suggested that quality of Paired Reading technique is not necessarily related to reading test gains of individual subjects.

Process studies have shown very variable degrees of conformity to the Paired Reading technique in different projects and different schools. However, in most studies there is evidence that training does result in some changes in tutor behaviour in the required direction. In larger, field studies of parent tutoring of Paired Reading, conformity to good practice has varied from 75 to 43 per cent of participants.

Studies of reading style have mostly shown that involvement in Paired Reading is associated with a reduction in error rate and refusal rate, and an increase in the use of context and self-correction. There is evidence that phonic skills also increase. Rate or speed of reading has usually been found to increase, although studies using the Neale measure of rate have also found decreases on occasion.

There is a relative paucity of follow-up data, those that are available relating to follow-up periods ranging from 4 weeks to 1 year. Again, results are various and seem to depend upon the individual project or school, but overall there is little evidence of Paired Reading gains being 'washed-out' by subsequent deceleration to below 'normal' rates. In some projects, Paired Readers continued to make accelerated rates of gain after the end of the intensive period for as long as 6 months, especially where tutoring continued. Even where the follow-up was over a period of as long as a year and rates of gain during the follow-up period were below 'normal', participant rates of gain were nevertheless better than those of control subjects. There is also some evidence that changes in reading style resulting from Paired Reading involvement can endure for as long as 1 year.

Large-Scale Field-Study Data

Small-scale studies which are reported in the published literature might not be a true reflection of 'real life'. Those enthusiastic enough to seek and achieve publication are not a random sample of all professionals who have tried Paired Reading. The published literature might, therefore, give a false picture of the likelihood of Paired Reading working in the average school with an average teacher, children and parents.

It is, therefore, valuable to compare the outcomes of Paired Reading which have been published to those in a large sample of such projects operated in one Local Education Authority. Of course, these results are still not completely unselected and perfectly representative, since operating a project was voluntary and not all teachers and schools did so. However, teachers are never likely to be forced to operate a project, so these results are representative of a very large number (and thus high proportion) of teachers who chose to do so.

In 1983 the Kirklees Local Education Authority (School District) established a project to help schools and other agencies to train, guide and support parents in the use of the Paired Reading technique. The services offered to schools and other intermediate dissemination agencies included briefing for professional staff, planning consultation, training sessions for parents and children, materials for training and evaluations, finance to defray the expenses of teachers making home visits in the evening, general support and review meetings, and arranging other kinds of assistance.

The Kirklees LEA comprises some 240 schools, and is within the most disadvantaged quartile of school districts in England, as indicated by census data. The participating children represented the full range of socio-economic status in the district. The majority of schools availed themselves fully of the support services available. Thus the majority of projects tended to follow a similar mode.

A first Paired Reading project usually started with a small group of children of a range of reading ability, who were closely supported and monitored.

It was typical for family pairs to contract into involvement for 5 sessions a week of at least 5 minutes during an initial intensive period of 8–9 weeks. In fact, the average family pair read for more than twice this amount of time during each session.

Monitoring of tutoring took various forms. In the case of parental involvement, many schools used a simple home–school diary. Some schools added 'booster' meetings in school. About a quarter of the total number of projects were supported by home visits by teachers, particularly where the parents were hard to reach or had other difficulties, or the children had a chronic reading problem. These were universally welcomed by parents and children alike. It was very rare for home visits to be seen as an intrusion in any kind of neighbourhood. All projects included feedback meetings and individual decisions about continuation.

The numerical data from the Kirklees research are too voluminous to include here – for further details, see Topping (1990), Topping and Whiteley (1990, 1993), Topping (1992a, 1992b) and Topping and Lindsay (1992a, 1992c). The data are also lodged in the ESRC Data Archive at the University of Essex in the UK, from where they are available in various electronic media for anyone interested in further analysis. The major conclusions are listed below:

1   From 1985 to 1987, 83 schools of all types operated 185 projects. Norm-referenced reading accuracy data were generated by 155 projects in 71 schools involving 2,372 children, 54 per cent of which were known to be boys and 42 per cent girls. 'Comprehension' data were available for 690 children. Data from separate projects were pooled.

2   The average period of intensive activity in projects was 8.62 weeks, the average baseline period in 23 baselined projects was 19.23 weeks (with great variability), and the average follow-up period in 17 follow-up projects was 25.85 weeks (with great variability). Comparison ('control') groups were a feature of 37 projects.

3   The majority of participants (74.8 per cent) were parent tutored, 7.8 per cent were same-age peer tutored and 6.3 per cent cross-age peer tutored. Other tutors were adult volunteers, teacher volunteers or unrecorded.

4   Home visits were incorporated into 26.5 per cent of projects, equally divided between less than one visit per child per project, between one and two visits per child, and greater than two.

5   Home–school reading diary cards from approximately 600 families were analysed, showing the mean frequency of reading per week to be 4.97 times and the total reading time during the project's intensive period to be 7 hours 13 minutes, the former statistic probably being more accurate.

6   Of 261 statistical analyses on the data, 56 per cent achieved non-parametric statistical significance, which is not to assume educational significance.

7   Results were analysed in terms of gain in reading age, but there was little sign of regression to the mean operating in reading accuracy data, although this may have occurred to a limited extent with the more erratic comprehension data and to a degree in some of the follow-up data.

8   The mean pre-post gain in reading accuracy was 6.97 months of reading age, and in comprehension 9.23 months. The ratio gain was 3.27 for accuracy and 4.39 for comprehension. As comprehension scores are more erratic and comprehension not readily differentiated from accuracy, this difference is not meaningful.

9   In 23 baselined projects incorporating 374 participants, of whom 288 were baselined children, baseline ratio gain for accuracy was 1.37 while pre-post ratio gain was 2.56, a highly statistically significant difference. In comprehension, both baseline and pre-post gains were high and the difference not statistically significant.

10 In 37 comparison ('control') group studies incorporating 580 participant and 446 comparison children, the scores in both accuracy and comprehension for participant children were statistically significantly greater than those for comparison children.

11 At short-term follow-up (equal to or less than 17 weeks), 102 children in 7 projects averaged ratio gains over the follow-up period of 2.01 for accuracy and 2.32 for comprehension.

12 At long-term follow-up (greater than 17 weeks), 170 children in 10 projects averaged ratio gains over the follow-up period of 1.20 in accuracy and 1.36 in comprehension.

13 Follow-up ratio gain did not correlate to a statistically significant degree with the length of follow-up period (coefficient 0.36, $p = 0.20$).

14 Where follow-up data are available in comparison-group projects, follow-up gains in reading accuracy show no statistically significant difference between participant and comparison groups. Thus, one may expect participants to remain relatively advantaged compared to non-participants, as relative pre-post gains are sustained in the long run although relative acceleration is not.

15 Follow-up ratio gains show no significant correlation with presence or otherwise of home visits, socio-economic status of catchment area or degree of retardation of participants. However, there is a significant correlation with pre-post gains, i.e. children doing best during the intensive period also do best at follow-up.

16 The follow-up data for peer tutoring are less encouraging than those for parent tutoring, but as yet they are sparse.

17 Overall effect sizes for reading accuracy were +0.87 and for comprehension +0.77.

18 Type and size of school showed little relationship with size of gains. Older children tended to show slightly higher gains in reading accuracy, but this is not educationally significant given the structure of reading tests.

19 The Spring term was the most popular for the operation of projects but the Autumn term yielded statistically significantly better results. The least popular Summer term yielded acceptable results in reading accuracy.

20 Projects rated as of better organizational quality yielded higher pre-post gains in reading accuracy. There was little evidence that a school's increasing experience in operating projects (associated with reducing novelty) had any significant influence on gains in reading accuracy.

21 Children from all social classes were involved in projects, 60 per cent of participants being of below-average socio-economic status for the LEA. There was a tendency for participants of lower socio-economic status to make larger gains in reading accuracy, even if not home visited. However, home visiting made an additional significant positive difference for participants in the lowest quartile of socio-economic status. There are implications here for the cost-effectiveness of differential inclusion of home-visiting support in this kind of service delivery.

22 A tendency was evident for more retarded readers to make larger gains in accuracy and comprehension, although this was small and in any event retardation (and reduction therein) has different implications at different basal reading ages.

23 At pre-test, on average girls were ahead of boys in accuracy and boys ahead of girls in comprehension. Boys made bigger gains than girls in accuracy and comprehension, but not statistically significantly. In comparison group projects, male participants made gains statistically significantly larger than those of controls, but females did not.

24 Participants of South Asian origin were recorded in 50 projects yielding norm-referenced data, operated in 30 schools. The average number of such participants in these projects was 5 (range 1–47, maximum proportion 74 per cent). Asian participants constituted 9.4 per cent of total participants, compared to 15.4 per cent in the total schoolchild population.

At pretest, Asians were behind whites, on average, in accuracy and comprehension. Asians made gains greater than white participants in accuracy (but not statistically significantly) and significantly smaller gains in comprehension. However, there are doubts about the validity of direct comparison of gain size from different basal reading ages, the non-partialling of socio-economic status for Asian participants, and the cultural relevance of the reading tests. Pre-post gains of Asian participants were greater than those of non-participant children of any ethnic origin.

25 Pre–post gains in reading accuracy were similar for parent-tutored, same-age peer-tutored and cross-age peer-tutored participants. Adult volunteers and teacher volunteers tutored very small numbers of participants and teacher volunteers tended to tutor much weaker children.

26 Pre–post gains of peer tutors were greater than those of peer tutees in reading accuracy, but the difference was not statistically significant.

27 In peer–tutor projects, same-sex pairings were much more common than mixed-sex pairings. Boy same-sex pairings yielded significantly higher gains for tutors than did girl same-sex pairings, although no difference was evident in outcomes for tutees. There was a tendency for mixed-sex

combinations to be good for tutors but poor for tutees, in terms of test results.

28   Self-recorded frequency of reading and time spent reading showed no significant relation to reading accuracy gains. Although the validity of informal self-recording as a measure of time on task is in doubt, there is no evidence here that Paired Reading works merely by increasing time spent on reading.

29   Of the reading tests used, the Neale Analysis and Daniels and Diack Test 1 showed coherent, positive correlations with subjective feedback from parents, teachers and children and to a degree with self-reported frequency of reading. Other tests showed few positive correlations and the New Macmillan Reading Analysis and Holborn Tests showed very low coherence with other data.

30   As different reading tests are relevant to different chronological age ranges, direct comparison of gains on them is a dubious exercise. However, there was a tendency for group reading tests to show greater variability than individual reading tests, but not consistently higher or lower pre-post gains. Tests of similar type and construction produced very different results in some cases. Gains on particular tests showed no consistent relationship with the likelihood of practice effects from the structure of the test, the availability or otherwise of parallel forms or the reading age-range relevance of the instrument.

The Burt test, Neale Analysis and Daniels and Diack Test 1 yielded stable results, which tended to be average or above. The Holborn, Daniels and Diack Test 12 and the Primary Reading Test yielded stable results, which were average or below. The Neale Analysis and the Macmillan Tests produced very different results in both accuracy and comprehension, despite their similar structure. Very erratic results were evident on the Widespan Test and the Macmillan test, the former tending to average out very high and the latter very low. The Schonell and Salford Tests also tended to produce low gain scores.

31   Eighty-five projects used parental feedback questionnaires at the end of the intensive period, and of the 1,466 participating parents, 1,068 returned questionnaires (return rate 73 per cent). Greater confidence in reading in their children was reported by 78 per cent of parents. More than 70 per cent of parents also reported that children were now reading more widely, enjoying reading more, keeping a steadier flow and making fewer mistakes (i.e. were reading more accurately). Between 65 per cent and 70 per cent of parents stated children were now reading more in absolute volume, were understanding books more (i.e. showing better comprehension), and were more willing to read.

Sixty two per cent of parents reported that their children were now more interested in reading and were reading with more expression. A significant minority of parents felt their children were now behaving better at home and were happier at home (15 per cent, 19 per cent). Regarding continuation, 38 per cent of families intended to continue Paired Reading twice weekly, 33 per cent intended to continue five times weekly, 22 per cent intended to continue with some reading at home but using a different approach or technique, and 8 per cent intended to stop altogether.

Twenty-nine projects used teacher questionnaires referring to 430 children (return rate 91 per cent). Generally, teacher feedback was less positive than parent feedback, but this may partially be a function of a higher response rate and a slightly different questionnaire structure. Seventy per cent of teachers reported project participants were showing more confidence in reading in class. Greater accuracy in reading had been observed in 67 per cent of children. About two-thirds of participants were reading a greater amount and showing greater fluency in reading. Between 55 and 60 per cent of children showed better reading comprehension and more interest and pleasure in reading in class. Greater width of reading was demonstrated by 53 per cent of children, more willingness to read by 48 per cent of children, better pacing in reading by 45 per cent of children and greater expressiveness by 38 per cent of children. Thirty-seven per cent of children were reported to be showing better concentration and motivation in class and 14 per cent of children better behaviour generally in class.

Child feedback questionnaires were used by 57 projects, in which 692 children provided feedback (return rate 72 per cent). Some child questionnaires were completed at school, but many were taken home. The child questionnaire responses were the most positive of all. Improved skill at all kinds of reading was reported by 95 per cent of participant children, and 92 per cent reported now liking all reading better. The technique was felt to be 'easy to learn to do' by 87 per cent of children, and 83 per cent liked doing it. A wish to continue doing Paired Reading was reported by 70 per cent of the children (virtually identical to the continuation options reported by parents), and 90 per cent of the children said they would tell other people about Paired Reading.

Further details of the subjective feedback will be found in Topping and Whiteley (1990). Parent-tutored children tended to evaluate their experiences more positively than those tutored by peers, but the feedback for peer tutoring was still very positive. Feedback was obtained from tutors as well as tutees. That from same-age peer tutees was more positive than that from cross-age tutees, although there was little difference between that from the two kinds of peer tutors.

Comparison of Outcomes from Small and Large-Scale Studies

Brief comparison of outcomes from the large-scale field data and from the published small-scale research literature can now be made.

The field data incorporate norm-referenced results from 2,372 subjects in 155 projects, while all the literature taken together yields data on 1,012 subjects in 60 projects. Mean ratio gains cited in the literature tended to be somewhat higher than those found in the field (4.23 vs 3.27 for accuracy, 5.37 vs 4.39 for comprehension).

This is to be expected, given the positive bias in published results stemming from submission and publication policies. It is nevertheless most encouraging that in the field average results are so little behind those of published studies. The Paired Reading technique combined with support services seems associated with a substantial degree of generalizability, replicability and durability.

Comparison of mean ratio gains in control/comparison group projects is of interest. In the literature are results from 19 control group projects incorporating some 300 subjects. In the field, data are available from twice this number of 'control' group projects, incorporating almost twice as many subjects. Again, the results from the literature are somewhat more positive than those from the field, literature experimentals tending to do better than field experimentals and literature controls tending to do less well than the field controls. This difference is less marked for comprehension data.

The tendency for literature outcomes to be better than field outcomes is more pronounced when considering effect sizes. In reading accuracy, the literature mean effect size is more than twice that for the field. This undoubtedly reflects greater variability within the field projects as well as smaller absolute gains. Again, this difference is less marked for reading comprehension.

The field study added substantially to the research literature with respect to follow-up data. In the literature, follow-up gains were cited from only five projects and these varied greatly. Some follow-up ratio gains were less than 1 but greater than control groups. Full data were not always cited. By contrast, the field research gives follow-up data on 17 projects, indicating mean short-term follow-up ratio gains in reading accuracy and comprehension of greater than 2, and in the longer term of 1.20 in accuracy and 1.36 in comprehension. The field follow-up data are thus considerably more substantial and encouraging.

Discussion and Conclusions

In recent years, there has been a movement away from the notion of the single, perfect experiment to methods of detecting general trends from many studies with the same focus. This has been coupled with a long overdue growth in concern for replication and generalization. Research in the real world almost inevitably implies imperfections, however.

Many of the studies and field trials reviewed above are riddled with methodological weaknesses. Participant self-selection in these studies may invalidate generalization of the results to all possible schools, classes and parent and peer tutors, especially if participation becomes persuaded or required rather than voluntary. The reading tests used in the studies reviewed were numerous, very various in type, and even more various in terms of the adequacy of information on norms, reliability and validity. Furthermore, they may have been administered by different testers in slightly different ways. Even where parallel forms were used, format practice effects may have occurred. The use of 'multiple measures of independent imperfection' may be no greater a methodological weakness than over-reliance on a single measure of purported reputability, however.

A further problem with many studies is that supposed 'control' groups were very rarely the result of random assignment to conditions, self-selection to non-participate being the most common feature of purported 'controls'. However, it is unsurprising that teachers felt unable to assign parents randomly to conditions, and more adequate control groups are found in some peer-tutoring studies. In some studies, it is not even clear what supposedly 'Paired Reading' technique tutors were trained in.

Beyond this, many of the studies are severely lacking in detailed process data. Although self-reported information on frequency and time spent reading was collected, its reliability might be questioned. More importantly, the time might not have been spent doing Paired Reading as trained. What evidence is available shows that the proportion of subjects who do Paired Reading 'properly' can vary greatly from study to study. Collecting and analysing process data on a large scale is very time consuming but a crude input–output model of evaluation is clearly less than satisfactory. In the longer run, more detailed studies of process to elucidate which aspects of Paired Reading are responsible for which aspects of outcome will prove most valuable.

Some of the studies reviewed have already considered the importance of the Reading Together component, which appears to be important in peer tutoring at least. However, there are aspects within Reading Together that may be further partialled – is the tutor modelling important or is it the supportive aspect which has most impact? Likewise, there is some evidence that the Paired Reading error-correction procedure has important effects in peer-tutoring applications, but it is not known whether this is also true of parent-tutored applications or whether alternative error-correction procedures would be equally or more potent.

It is also relevant to raise the issue of variability in quantity and quality of monitoring and follow-up support. This monitoring clearly needs to be formative as well as summative. Supposedly comparative studies which assert that Paired Reading is not better than alternative treatments, when it is clear that Paired Reading was not actually carried out but was merely the content of patently ineffective training, are not helpful. One or two studies have deliberately manipulated degree of follow-up as a variable, usually finding no statistically significant differences with small samples. The field data suggest that the incorporation of home visiting does tend to improve norm-referenced outcomes. Home visiting is a time-consuming and therefore expensive input, however, so issues of cost-effectiveness arise alongside issues of absolute effectiveness.

Beyond this, there are implications for further research that might seek to identify interactions between treatment and participant types. It would be naive and potentially damaging to seek a uniformly and ubiquitously 'best' technique in comparative studies. While Paired Reading has demonstrated a high degree of durability, replicability and generalizability, alternative techniques or modifications of Paired Reading may prove to be more effective with specific sub-populations of target subjects. Equally, the effects of the application of different techniques sequentially must be explored, possibly with a view towards discerning some developmental schema for deployment of different techniques.

In this context, it must be noted that although the comparative studies reviewed tend to favour Paired Reading, such small-sample studies represent only one approach to exploring these issues. Alternatively, a meta-analytic approach to comparison could be pursued, comparing effect sizes in all Paired Reading studies with effect sizes in all studies using each specific alternative technique.

Most of the small-sample, directly comparative studies yielding statistically significant differences have found Paired Reading to be more effective than 'Hearing' or 'Listening'. Attempts to meta-analyse the literature on studies of 'hearing' or 'listening' approaches quickly run into difficulties, however. Of the major studies in the UK, one (Hewison and Tizard 1980) found statistically significant effects, sustained at follow-up, while the other (Hannon 1987) failed to find statistically significant effects.

Unfortunately, a very large proportion of the other literature on 'hearing/listening' approaches fails to offer a precise description of what tutors were asked to do or actually did, and numerical outcome data are often conspicuous by their absence. However, crudely aggregating the 14 published 'hearing/listening' studies where reading age data are given (total n=290) yields an average pre-post ratio gain of 2.53 compared to the Paired Reading literature average of 4.23 and the Paired Reading field average of 3.27.

Recommendations for further research include more multiple-site field trials of improved quality. This is beginning to occur in an international context. Both comparative and meta-analytic studies of generalization over settings, target groups of various characteristics and contexts of variable resourcing and support are needed. Studies should include control and/or alternative treatment groups and allocate subjects randomly to conditions wherever possible, while seeking to ensure similar levels of subject motivation and commitment, and of amount of reading practice across conditions. Avoidance of group contamination is essential.

More valid and reliable outcome measures should be sought, and the use of reading age gain and ratio gain scores preferably should be avoided. However, this may only be achieved at the cost of losing comparability with the previous literature. Use of adequate control groups and the citing of statistical significance in reference to these would enable the application of alternative forms of meta-analysis. Further studies need to specify exactly the training content and the training, monitoring and follow-up formats used. Detailed process data on conformity to trained method should be collected, especially in comparative studies, without reliance on subject self-reportage.

Further studies systematically manipulating aspects of the Paired Reading technique for the purpose of comparative evaluation are required, and this could also be pursued with reference to training, monitoring and follow-up formats to determine the most cost-effective methods with differing target groups. Furthermore, long-term follow-up studies including detailed process data will need to be conducted on all of these permutations, as some methods may prove less self-sustaining or resistant to distortion than others.

Returning to the *status quo*, however, it may be concluded that despite serious methodological weakness in many of the studies, the better-quality studies have shown no less encouraging results than the rest. In any event the sheer volume of multiple-site replication is impressive. Paired Reading has certainly been better evaluated than many educational innovations.

It has been argued that community interventions should be: (i) simple, (ii) inexpensive, (iii) effective, (iv) compatible with the existing values and need structures of the population, (v) flexible, (vi) decentralized, and (vii) sustainable. The research on Paired Reading reviewed here is encouraging and suggests that in a context of well-organized service delivery the technique is capable of meeting at least requirements i–vi. Conclusions on the last requirement must await further longer-term follow-up studies.

CHAPTER 5

How to Evaluate Paired Reading Projects

Considerable emphasis has been placed on evaluating Paired Reading projects. Just because spectacular results have been achieved in some places, that doesn't guarantee you will get them right there where you are.

Especially with your first effort, you need to know how successful you have been and how you can improve effectiveness even more in the future.

Then circumstances will change or you will want to do something a little differently, so evaluation remains essential – a continuous cycle. Evaluation will help convince sceptics of the value of what you are doing. Carrying out your own evaluation is a lot more comfortable than some outsider imposing it upon you. You will also find the parents and children very eager to be told how well they've done – so you'd better have something concrete to tell them!

One of the great virtues of Paired Reading is its cost-effectiveness, i.e. what the child gets out for the time and effort the child, parent(s) and teacher put in. So it would be nonsensical to spend a vast amount of time evaluating a project. However, a small amount of time is worth devoting to this task. This chapter details some of the ways of going about it. You will need to choose the ways you think are best and easiest for your own situation.

First, you need to think clearly about planning your evaluation design.

Evaluation Design

The obvious thing is to apply some measure(s) like a reading test at the start of the project and again at the end of the project to the children who take part (Pre- and Post-Test Design). But if your measure is not norm-referenced (standardized), you will have no way of telling whether the children would have made the pre–post changes anyway, irrespective of the project.

Even if your measure is norm-referenced (standardized), unless your results are spectacularly better than 'normal' rates of gain, you still won't have convincing evidence that the children could only have made those gains with the help of the project.

Standardizations refer to averages for hundreds of children from all over the country. However, the standardization may not be immediately relevant to a small group of children with peculiar reading in your particular school. So you really need to compare the progress of your project children with the progress of a similar local group who have not been involved in the project.

If you offer involvement in the project to twenty children, and only 10 finally participate, you can use the ten 'drop-outs' as a 'comparison' group. But the ten drop-outs are not a true 'control' group, because they have self-selected not to participate, and factors which incline them to do that are likely to be associated with factors causing their reading difficulties. Nevertheless it is better to have a comparison group than not, so you should apply your measure(s) pre- and post-project to both groups. Don't try to make out your comparison group is a true control group, though.

To get a true control group, you would have to list your twenty children, then allocate them randomly to 'control' or 'project' groups (by tossing a coin or using random number tables). Both groups would be pretested, then only the 'project' group invited to participate. However, not all of them would agree, so then you would have:

Control Group	Experimental Group
n=10	Participating n=5
	Not Participating n=5

After post-testing all twenty at the end of the project, what comparisons can you make? Strictly speaking, you should compare all the 'controls' with all the 'experimentals', whether the latter participated or not.

This builds in conservatism to any claims you might make based on the data, but does allow you to use quite stringent parametric tests of statistical significance without invalidating their underlying assumptions. Alternatively, or in addition, you can make a three-way analysis comparing the three groups, but you will only be able to apply non-parametric tests of statistical significance.

In any event, the numbers quoted here in the experimental sub-groups are so small as to make comparisons of doubtful validity. A minimum sample size of ten is desirable to have any real confidence in your results.

So far we have talked about fairly classical research design. But there are alternative approaches, which can be as 'scientifically' acceptable (depending on the prejudices of who you are asking for an opinion!) These alternatives can prove easier to carry out, especially where existing data can be utilized.

For instance, if a school has a regular routine of applying reading tests, historical data some time into the past may be available for the project group. This enables you to scrutinize the fluctuations in progress in the past, and see how the gains during the project compare. This can be called the Baseline or Time Series Design. Where the regular trend of time series data is 'interrupted' by a special event like a Paired Reading project, you check to see what sort of a blip in the trend emerges.

Even better would be a Baseline or Time Series with Comparison Series. You might compare acceleration and development over time in the project group to that of other children in the year group. Again, remember this is a comparison group, not a control group. Your comparison group could be all the rest of the year group, children who were invited to participate in the project but refused, children with similar, more or less severe reading difficulty, or any other groups with whom comparison would be interesting and valid.

It is very advantageous if the Time Series can be continued after the end of the project. This will generate very interesting and valuable long-term follow-up data.

One of the problems with true control groups is that their use involves denying a service or facility to people who are in need of it, at least in the short run. You can justify this on the grounds that you do not have the resources to help everyone at the same time effectively anyhow, and random allocation is fairer than other methods of 'rationing'. It can also be argued that until you have demonstrated that the project has actually worked by using the control group, you don't know whether you are denying the control group anything worthwhile.

Where a limited amount of a service or facility is available, there is often felt to be a moral obligation that all the children in greatest need receive the service. If enough service is available to meet the needs of those who are worst off, but still leave some spare capacity, the limited surplus service may be extended to the larger band of children whose needs are less severe. But how to allocate the limited surplus to this large group? Arguably, random selection for project inclusion is the fairest way to go about it for this mid-band of children.

If the project workers are unhappy with this, a fixed arbitrary criterion on some measure can be set to determine inclusion or non-inclusion for this mid-band, e.g. a specific and exact reading age. A design which becomes useful here is the Regression Discontinuity Design.

If you look at the relationship between pretest and post-test reading ages for the participant group (below the cut-off point) and the non-participant group (above the cut-off point), you would hope to find something like this:

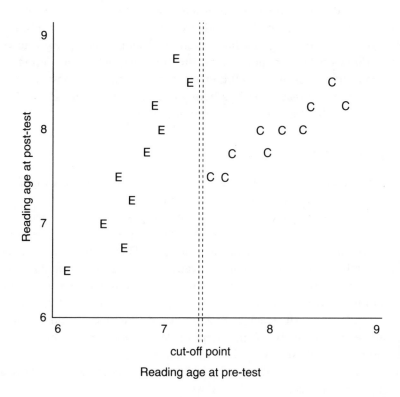

Figure 5.1
Regression discontinuity design

Finally, one further design is probably worth mentioning. This is the Multiple Baseline Design. If a larger group of potential clients exists than can be serviced at one time, they may have to be serviced by two consecutive projects. Where one half of the clients have to be serviced first, and the second later, it is reasonable and fair to allocate to 'early' and 'late' groups randomly.

Teachers will often do this when a whole class of (say) thirty wants to do Paired Reading but it is clear that there is not enough teacher time to look at thirty diary cards each week. It is better to work with half of the class properly at one time, rather than overload and stress the system. The 'late' group will be all the more enthusiastic for having their appetite whetted. Quite often the late group make bigger gains than the 'early' group.

So in the short term you compare the gains of the participant early group to those of the non-participant late comparison group. In the medium term you compare the gains of the now participant late group to their own progress before participating, and to the progress of the early group when participating. You can also collect post-participation follow-up data on the early group and compare it to their own gains while participating. In the longer term you can collect post-participation follow-up data on the late group and compare it to the follow-up data on the early group as well as to their own participation gains. You can also collect longer-term follow-up data on the early group and compare that to their shorter-term follow-up data. Try drawing this on a graph of time against reading test scores.

If you want to get really complicated, you could combine features of these designs. Other, usually more complex, designs are also possible. Whatever you choose to do, some attempt to guard against the 'Hawthorne Effect' is necessary. This is the effect whereby the subjects of a study show brief improvement purely because some attention is being paid to them and there is some element of novelty about the proceedings, quite irrespective of the actual nature of the intervention.

Another possible source of embarrassment is the 'John Henry Effect' – where the control group, alerted to the fact that somebody considers them to be in need but is not providing anything for them, determines to improve anyway, and does so without apparent outside intervention.

A word about the necessity for long-term follow-up is necessary. Readers may be familiar with the substantial body of evidence which details how gains produced by specialist 'remedial' teaching in school often 'wash out' in comparison to control groups at follow-up two or more years after termination of the tuition. Paired Reading seems to be less prone to this effect, but this needs demonstrating project by project wherever possible. The gathering of routine time series data in school may permit this without undue expenditure of energy.

Types of Evaluation

There are two main types of evaluation, 'process' (or formative) evaluation and 'product' (or summative or outcome) evaluation.

Summative evaluation looks solely at the end-product of a project, without looking closely at how effective each of the various aspects of the organization and methods of the project were in achieving this goal. These latter questions are the focus of formative evaluation, so named because the data gathered enable you to re-form a better project next time, or even adjust the current one as you go along.

As part of formative evaluation, the opinions and observations of all participants as to the effectiveness of the teaching and support methods used could be solicited as you go along. Alternatively (or in addition) detail an 'independent' observer to record observations *in situ* according to some structured format or check list. However, this takes time and the effect of the presence of the observer, especially in small group settings, has to be reckoned with.

The Paired Reading Check List (PRR8) is a useful tool for formative evaluation, either by participant observation on home visits or as a self-evaluation check by parents and children themselves. The Home–School Reading Diary (PRR6) also gives process data about frequency and content of reading. Keep a note of attendance at 'booster' meetings, how many home visits are made and to whom, and so on. Remember that process evaluation is not just about how well *they* are doing their bit – it is about how well *everyone* is doing their bit.

The section on 'Measures' below will inevitably mainly focus on project end-products, although some of the methods discussed will throw some tangential light on processes involved.

Measures

There are various basic requirements of any measures you seek to use. Economy of cost in materials and of time in administration and scoring are two obvious considerations. The measure needs to be reliable, in the sense of not being susceptible to wild random fluctuations or erratic guesswork. It also needs to be valid, i.e. one must be assured that it actually measures what it is purporting to measure. Of equal importance, it needs to be relevant to the processes in question. Thus a phonic skills teaching programme would probably not be relevantly evaluated by application of a reading test containing a very high proportion of irregular 'sight' words.

Last, but by no means least, the measure must generate information which is analysable. A vast quantity of impressionistic opinion or observation may be fascinating to the project organizers, but will not enable them to communicate their findings to others in a clear and credible way. These considerations are worth bearing in mind irrespective of the type(s) of measure chosen, which we can now consider, category by category.

Individual standardized tests

None of the popular individual standardized or norm-referenced reading tests has proved entirely satisfactory for evaluating Paired Reading projects.

Word recognition tests (such as the Burt, Schonell and Macmillan Graded Word Recognition Test in the UK) fall down on the question of relevance. An intervention method which revolves around promoting the use of contextual clues is not likely to be relevantly evaluated by reading tests which provide no context. Nevertheless, sheer increased exposure to print does tend to result in greater accuracy on common 'sight' words, and post-project gains on these tests may be expected. However, they can be expected to be smaller than on tests which provide a context and focus on comprehension as well. This is despite the fact that word recognition tests are particularly prone to 'practice effects' – scores inflated by familiarity with the test items. Few of them have parallel forms to ameliorate this problem.

A more meaningful option seems to be offered by the various sentence reading tests, which do contain some context, albeit fragmentary. Unfortunately, some of these are very brief, which may partially account for their popularity. (Examples in the UK include the Holborn, Salford and Hertfordshire Tests.) Few have been produced in recent years and in the older ones the language is now dated, and the relevance of the standardization even more in doubt. Some have parallel forms (e.g. the Salford, which also has a more recent standardization). In too many cases, the standardization suffers from being highly localized and some of the tests cover only a narrow age range. Where the test is extremely brief (e.g. thirteen sentences in the Salford), small changes in correct response generate large shifts in standardized scores.

An interesting variant are tests which require children to read questions out loud and then give the answer. An example in the UK is the Daniels and Diack Test 1, often used for evaluating Paired Reading projects with younger pupils. It does allow the tester to generate a game-like, purposive and meaningful aura to the operation, which must add to the test's relevance for evaluating Paired Reading projects. However, this test has a bias towards the overinclusion of phonically regular words. This may have a curious effect on results.

This test also well illustrates the need to check information in the test manual. You should always do this, and may find that there has never been adequate information about its standardization, which must therefore be suspect.

The standardization given for this test does allow some discrimination between children at very early stages of reading development (5 to 7 years), but is of little use after 8 years. Ideally you need to find a test which not only covers all the wide range of reading competency in your project and control groups, but which will still be relevant when you are collecting follow-up data in a year's time. Beware of tests which appear to do this but actually suffer from a 'ceiling' or 'floor' effect. They may include many items covering a part of the total span they purport to cover, but very few items at the extremes. So children with a high pretest score have little scope to better it, while at the other extreme many children may be given the same very low (or 'below scale') score when they are actually quite different in reading competence.

The most popular individual test for evaluating Paired Reading projects has been the Neale Analysis of Reading Ability, originated in Australia and now re-standardized there and in the UK in its second edition. This requires children to read continuous passages of meaningful prose accompanied by an illustration, followed by aural questions to check understanding. This kind of test is much more like real reading. Despite being rather time consuming, it provides a continuous context and separate scores for Accuracy, Comprehension and Rate of reading. It covers a fairly wide age range, and on the surface seems the most relevant test to the Paired Reading process.

Much of the evaluation data cited in Chapter 4 used the Neale Analysis in its first edition. Unfortunately, this edition was fraught with doubts and inconsistencies. Some of the language was very dated ('the milkman's horse' featured) and was set in a narrow cultural framework. The standardization was localized and out of date. The data on reliability and validity was based on very small numbers. The assessment of Rate was of particularly low reliability. The comprehension questions were few in number, resulting in the response to one question potentially effecting a substantial shift in score. Many project evaluations have demonstrated much bigger gains in Comprehension than in Accuracy, and in some cases the gains in Comprehension have been so large as to be barely credible.

Furthermore, there are grave doubts about the cross-reliability of the supposedly 'parallel' Neale forms A, B and C. Of the children involved in the original standardization, the majority completed form A. The evidence for the comparability of forms B and C is thus based on very small numbers indeed. Some evaluators have tried to get round this by allocating forms at random at pretest and at random from the remaining two at post-test. Even this procedure has not eliminated all the improbable eccentricities from the use of the Neale Analysis however.

The alternative was to pre- and post-test on form A, the best standardized form. There is some evidence that the Neale Analysis does not suffer from practice effects nearly so badly as word recognition tests, at least over periods of 15 weeks and 1 year, but whether this applies with periods as short as 6 weeks, and with the non-normal samples at which Paired Reading projects are often aimed, is another question. Finally, the original Neale standardization utilized children only in the 7–11-year-age range, so its use on children outside this age bracket is invalid, although its use with older children seems quite common.

Having said all this, the second edition of the Neale Analysis has rectified some, but not all, of these defects. For the purpose of evaluating Paired Reading projects, the Neale Analysis may still be the best. Similar tests are now available from other publishers (e.g. the New Macmillan Reading Analysis in the UK), but should all be carefully scrutinized. (While the NMRA has up-to-date content and standardization, it is very locally standardized on only a small sample and tends to give very erratic results.)

Group standardized tests

Many group standardized tests have a Cloze or sentence-completion aspect, and thus to some extent 'automatically' assess comprehension. However, Paired Reading is an oral, individual and relational method, based on children following their own interests, and none of these aspects is reflected in a group reading test.

It can be argued that if Paired Reading 'works', it should raise reading skills in areas and situations not directly involved in the method itself. In other words, that gains from Paired Reading should generalize to different kinds of reading content and situations. Of course, a poor result may be taken as a sign of a poor test as much as one of non-impact of Paired Reading.

Whatever the reliability quoted in the manual, with a small and idiosyncratically selected group of children with reading difficulties, reliability may not be good.

Where group and individual tests have been used in parallel to evaluate a project, the correlation between the two kinds of test result has often been poor. Use of group reading tests may show substantial rates of gain taking the project group as a whole, but the results for individual children may seem very doubtful. Even more reason not to give exact figures to families who may attach too much importance to them!

As with individual tests, there may be problems of age range coverage (e.g. in the UK the London Test only covers 10–12-year-olds). The Wide-Span Reading Test tries to solve this problem, but is very complicated to take and administer. Some group reading tests are massively thorough (e.g. the Edinburgh Reading Tests in the UK), and tap the reading process in a variety of ways, but are very time-consuming, expensive and overwhelming for weak readers. (The 'short form' of the Edinburgh Test is still very large and is only standardized for 10–11-year-olds.

Also now available is a group reading test which requires the subjects to read a real book before doing a test based on it. However, it seems likely that the best use of group reading tests will still be to monitor overall standards in large populations.

Non-standardized tests

Tests that are not referred to some standard notion of what the average child should be able to do instead refer the testee's performance to some fixed *criterion* of competence. These tests are often closely related to, or taken from, curricular materials also used in teaching the child. Hence these tests are also known as criterion-referenced or curriculum-based tests.

The advantage of non-standardized tests is that they can much more flexibly reflect the reality of the school curriculum, if not so easily the Paired Reading process as it occurs in the home. Their disadvantage is that comparison with national norms is no longer possible, and the absence of that vast, distant quasi-'control' group means that much more emphasis must be placed on achieving an adequate evaluation design.

An Informal Reading Inventory provides an excellent vehicle for assessing children's reading competence, in terms of point of functioning at Independence Level (99 per cent Accuracy, 90 per cent Comprehension), Instructional Level (95 per cent Accuracy, 75 per cent Comprehension) and Frustration Level (90 per cent or less Accuracy, 50 per cent or less Comprehension). The Inventory is likely to be based on the school's core reading scheme, or some other sequential material such as the SRA Reading Laboratory.

A typical inventory would have 10 to 20 passages selected from consecutive main readers, with associated comprehension questions. Unfortunately IRIs are fairly time-consuming to devise and administer (although some Teacher Resource Centres provide them off-the-shelf for the most popular reading schemes), and they are not based on the child's own interests. However, they are much more like 'real' reading. The results of a Paired Reading project evaluated by an IRI would not, of course, be readily comparable to those of another school using an IRI based on a different curriculum or reading scheme.

An alternative possibility is some kind of Cloze test based, again, most usually on the core reading scheme. A series of passages from consecutive readers are reproduced with some words deleted. The deletions can be of a predominantly syntactic or semantic nature, a combination of both, or be random. The children have to supply the missing words. If the exercise is done on a silent reading basis, which is the more common, no emphasis is placed on spelling correctness. The disadvantages of IRIs are shared by Cloze tests. Cloze tests on a silent reading basis involve less actual time expenditure by the tester, but yield less useful information.

A further possibility is to construct a word recognition test from the Dolch, Edwards or more recent lists of the most commonly occurring (high-frequency) words. Much the same exercise could be carried out using items of vocabulary from the school's core reading scheme. Scoring could be in terms of how many words the child could read correctly in a given time span, or in terms of number of words read correctly out of a given set of words. There are different views about whether reading faster is necessarily a good thing, but speeded tests may be worth a try as a measure of fluency on vocabulary which should be familiar. Some of the comments made about standardized word recognition tests also apply here.

Diagnostic tests

Some attainment tests include a 'diagnostic' element, most usually some form of miscue or error analysis. Both individual and group tests do this.

Miscue analysis is a useful tool for teachers to incorporate in daily practice, but can be fairly time-consuming, especially until you are really fluent at doing it. Paired Reading is thought to work partly by increasing children's usage of contextual cues and there is evidence that this does occur.

Other kinds of diagnostic tests attempt to measure supposed 'sub-skills' which are assumed to underlie the development of reading ability. The Illinois Test of Psycholinguistic Abilities (USA) and the Aston Index (UK) are examples of this approach, attempting to tap 'sub-skills' such as auditory sequential memory, visual reversal discrimination, and so forth. However, evidence for the real existence of these theoretical sub-skill constructs is not easy to find.

Some sub-skill test scores correlate moderately well with reading ability but causative linkages cannot be proven. Others correlate very poorly. Nor is there much evidence that training pupils in these sub-skills consequently improves their reading, although it does raise their scores on tests of sub-skills. It is difficult to relate the sub-skills theories to the theoretical model of how Paired Reading works. It is thus difficult to generate hypotheses as to what effect Paired Reading could be expected to have on sub-skill test scores. On the whole, there does not appear to be much mileage in the use of this kind of diagnostic test for evaluating Paired Reading projects, particularly in view of their extremely time-consuming nature.

Diagnosis or assessment of phonic skills, for all its usefulness in classroom teaching, likewise appears to have little place in the evaluation of Paired Reading, since the theoretical connections between the phonic method of learning to read and the Paired Reading method seem tenuous, although the two approaches are complementary. It is possible that the increased fluency of reading characteristically stemming from the Paired Reading method serves to increase speed of sub-vocal phonic analysis and synthesis on words of intermediate length and difficulty, but this is pure speculation.

Miscellaneous assessments

The possibilities for assessing other variables of greater or less degrees of apparent relevance to the Paired Reading process are endless. Assessments of pupils' abstract understanding of what the reading process is, or is for, is possible using Clay's 'Concepts about Print' (Clay, 1979) or Downing's 'Linguistic Awareness in Reading Readiness' (Downing et al., 1993) scales, for instance. Again it is less than clear how this could be related to the theoretical model of how Paired Reading operates.

A variety of 'Attitude to Reading' scales are available, but many are long and complex paper-and-pencil exercises of doubtful relevance and limited specificity, quite apart from the considerations of reliability and validity.

A significant number of investigators have included a pre–post measure of understanding of meaning of words, on the assumption that more reading produces wider vocabularies, and positive gains have indeed been demonstrated in comparison to control groups. On the same principle, spelling ability might be expected to improve and general knowledge to expand, but this has yet to be demonstrated.

The socio-emotional aspects of Paired Reading are highly significant, and attempts can be made to tap these by some form of measure. However, the very complexity and intangibility of the socio-emotional factors involved render them difficult to reveal on paper-and-pencil measures. One study which demonstrated substantial gains in reading attainments among the project children also found the children seemed to have worse 'self-images' – as indicated by a paper-and-pencil test – a somewhat improbable result.

Improvement in behaviour at home and at school are not infrequently reported by parents and teachers as a result of Paired Reading involvement. This is likely to be difficult to capture on some form of behavioural check list (such as the Bristol Social Adjustment Guides in the UK), which are in any event only a somewhat more structured form of participant observation.

Structured Observation and Feedback

The views of the major participants in the project (children, parents, teachers) should always be elicited in some way. To rely simply on primitive instruments such as tests is to risk missing the texture of the reality of what happened. The participants will probably offer more process insights than summative conclusions, but the former must not be neglected. Formulating and communicating opinions serve not only to gather information, but also to clarify the participant's mind on the subject, resolve any residual practical problems, and very often to recharge and commit the participants to continued effort.

A group meeting for all participants at the end of the initial period is often a good idea. This could be (audio-) tape-recorded for more detailed analysis later (although an analysis of such data could prove a massive task). If time is available, individual interviews with at least the parents along some semi-structured format is desirable, perhaps in the context of the last home visit if these are taking place. Similar interviews with the children and teachers are desirable, but probably need carrying out by an 'outsider' to the project if they are to be remotely objective. Perhaps a student could be deployed to undertake this as a piece of field research.

Realistically, time constraints and/or the need to have readily analysable data often drive people into using some form of questionnaire. However, there are very large doubts about the reliability and validity of responses to paper-and-pencil tests, and other forms of data gathering should be carried out as well. In the construction of questionnaires, the project leaders or participants are best placed to decide which questions are important to them. However, the device must be structured to eliminate any possibility of leading respondents into giving a particular answer.

A multiple-choice format gives easily analysable data but is crude and simplistic, while an open-ended format is dependent on the free writing skills of the respondents and yields data which is often difficult to analyse. Reproducible Evaluation Questionnaires will be found in Part Four Section A (PRR9). These have the advantage of previous widespread use in at least one area in the UK, the results from which can be considered to form a crude kind of 'standardization' or norm-reference (see Topping and Whiteley 1990).

These simple devices relating to both process and summative issues can be completed separately or together by both parents and children. The Teacher Evaluation Questionnaire asks more specifically for the teachers' observations about changes in the child's reading behaviour in school during the course of the project. Where no relevant observations have been made, no response is required.

An important point is illustrated here, namely, the nebulosity of such notions as 'attitudes'. If you want people's feelings about the project, ask for them directly, but don't expect them necessarily to bear much relationship to the participant's actual behaviour or even the children's progress in reading. On the other hand, if you want people's observations of what participants actually did, ask for that directly, giving a 'no observations made' option. But avoid confusing the two by asking for woolly, generalized 'attitudes' or 'opinions'.

Stability of Measures

Caveats about reliability and validity apply to all the aforementioned kinds of measures. Where a school is using a self-designed questionnaire, it is worthwhile 'piloting' it with a relevant sub-group in your own locality first. But don't assume that its stability (on a test–retest, no intervention basis) with a normal sample in your school will necessarily reflect its stability with a sub-sample of 'abnormal' readers. The best bet may be a test–retest no-intervention pilot run with the project group to give time series and/or reliability data specific to the situation prior to the project.

Where standardized or criterion-referenced tests are in use, pre- and post-project measures should ideally be carried out by the same person, to ensure that any bias (particularly to generosity in scoring) or other 'tester effects' will be the same on both occasions.

Analysis of Data

So far as statistical analysis is concerned, it has already been noted that the use of random allocation to samples usually permits the use of parametric methods (e.g. 't' tests), while non-random allocation usually implies the use of non-parametric methods (e.g. Wilcoxon Tests, Fisher Tests, Mann-Whitney Tests, Chi-squared Tests, etc.).

With random samples, an initial 'feel' for the data gained via a simple scattergram could be followed by an analysis of covariance (ANCOVA) to allow for any differences at pretest between experimental and control groups, followed by an analysis of variance (ANOVA), perhaps repeatedly. Correlation analysis is possible, and coefficients can subsequently be tested for statistical significance, but by and large this is a less 'powerful' procedure, raising greater doubts about the direction of causative linkages.

There is a great difference between statistical and educational significance, however. The larger your sample, the more likely you are to obtain statistical significance, other things being equal. So big gains for your Paired Readers compared to a control group may not be statistically significant if you only have five children in each group. On the other hand, if a very large Paired Reading project produces gains in the project group which compared to those in the control group are only just statistically significant at the 5 per cent probability level, searching questions need asking about the educational significance of the results. Was it worth all that time and effort for gains so small?

It should also be borne in mind that where a very large number of different outcome measures are used, the chances are that one or two will show statistically significant changes irrespective of any real impact of the project. Fortunately, Paired Reading projects do not usually find themselves in this area of doubt, since the majority of moderately well organized Paired Reading projects show gains of at least twice 'normal' rates of progress during the project, and the educational significance of this is rarely in doubt, even before more subjective feedback is considered.

For those unsure of their competence in statistical analysis, or doubting the validity of the procedures, simple comparison of raw data on scattergrams or graphing of shifts in averages for groups gives a ready visual indication of changes. Certainly the data is worth summarizing in this sort of way for feedback to the participants, who may be assumed to be statistically unsophisticated.

Evaluation Results Feedback

One of the disadvantages of complex data analysis is that it takes time, and very often early feedback of evaluation results to the project participants is highly desirable, to renew their commitment and recharge their energies. A simple graph and/or brief tables of average scores for the groups is probably the best vehicle for this – remember, the results must be understood by the children as well.

The unreliability of standardized tests makes giving individual test scores to individual families a risky business, and care must be taken throughout not to give undue emphasis to standardized test data as distinct from other types. Any individual test scores are best given in an individual interview rather than a group meeting situation, if given at all.

In any event it is best for one person to take the responsibility for collating and presenting the evaluation data, or it might lie about on scraps of paper for ever. Evaluation results have a number of other uses as well. Publicity via the local press, professional journals or education curriculum bulletins or in-service meetings not only helps to disseminate good practice and help more children, it also serves to boost the morale of the project initiators and participants.

The results may be useful to convince sceptics on the school staff, generate a wider interest and produce a more coherent future policy on parent involvement in the school. The school governors will be interested, as should be various LEA (School District) Officers (educational or school psychologists, advisers and administrators). A demonstration of cost-effectiveness may elicit more tangible support from administration or politicians. Associated services such as children's library services, reading and language centres, peripatetic remedial services, and so on, may be drawn into the network of community support by a convincing evaluation report.

So to the final word. If you get results you don't like, you'll spend hours puzzling over them trying to explain them away. Make sure that if you get results you do like, you spend as much time and energy searching for other factors outside the project that could have produced them. If you don't spot them, someone else might – and probably will!

References – Paired Reading

Items marked * have not been referred to specifically in the text, but may prove of interest. Many are descriptive and contain no evaluation.

Allington, R.L. (1980) Teacher interruption behaviours during primary-grade and oral reading, *Journal of Educational Psychology*, **72** (3), 371–7.

Atherley, C.A. (1989) 'Shared Reading' – an experiment in peer tutoring in the primary classroom, *Educational Studies*, **15**(2), 145–53.

Bamber, S. (1990) Peer tutoring, *Links*, **16**(1), 26–7.

Barrett, J. (1986) Reading with mother: a paired reading programme described and evaluated, *Reading (UKRA)*, **20**(3), 173–8.

   * (1987) Paired Reading; psycholinguistics in practice, *Reading (UKRA)*, **21**(3), 152–8.

* Booth, S. and Winter, J. (1987) Peer tutored Paired Reading in a college of further education, *Paired Reading Bulletin*, **3**, 2–5.

* Brailsford, A. (1991) Paired Reading: positive reading practice. A training videotape with manual. Edmonton, Alberta: North Alberta Reading Specialists' Council (distributed by the International Reading Association, Newark, DE).

* Bruce, P. (1985) Paired Reading with mixed ability middle infants, *Paired Reading Bulletin*, **1**, 5–9.

   * (1986) A peer tutoring project with a class of 9 and 10 Year Olds, *Paired Reading Bulletin*, **2**, 71–5.

* Bryans, T., Kidd, A. and Levey, M. (1985) The Kings Heath project, in Topping and Wolfendale (*op. cit.*).

Burdett, L. (1985) Parental involvement in reading: a comparative study of Paired Reading and Individualised Reading with poor readers. MEd thesis, University of Hong Kong.

   * (1986) A study of P.R. and Individualised Reading in Hong Kong, *Paired Reading Bulletin*, **2**, 53–60 (also in *British Journal of Special Education*, **13**(4), 151–4).

Burt, C. and Vernon, P.E. (1938) *Burt (Rearranged) Word Reading Test*. London: Hodder and Stoughton.

* Burton, F. (1988) Parental involvement in reading and language: developing and sustaining participation through a school pyramid, *Paired Reading Bulletin*, **4**, 1–6.

Bush, A.M. (1982) A 'Paired Reading' experiment involving parents in a multicultural educational priority area. Advanced Diploma dissertation, Leeds Polytechnic.

   (1983) Can pupils' reading be improved by involving their parents?, *Remedial Education*, **18**(4), 167–70.

   (1985) Paired Reading at Deighton Junior School, in Topping and Wolfendale (*op. cit.*).

   * (1987) Cross-age tutoring at Deighton, *Paired Reading Bulletin*, **3**, 16–23.

Bushell, R., Miller, A. and Robson, D. (1982) Parents as remedial teachers, *Journal of the Association of Educational Psychologists*, **5**(9), 7–13.

Butkowsky, I.S. and Willows, D.M. (1980) Cognitive-motivational characteristics of children varying in reading ability: evidence of learned helplessness in poor readers, *Journal of Educational Psychology*, **72**(3), 408–22.

Byron, D. (1987) *Parent/School Liaison: the Hartcliffe Comprehensive Paired Reading Project*. Bristol: Education Psychology Service, Hartcliffe.

Byron, D. and Brock, R. (1984) *Working with Parents: the Golden Valley Paired Reading Project*. Bristol: Educational Psychology Service, Hartcliffe.

Carrick-Smith, L. (1982) An investigation into the effectiveness of Paired Reading. MSc (Educational Psychology) thesis, University of Sheffield.

   * (1985) A research project in Paired Reading, in Topping and Wolfendale (*op. cit.*).

Cawood, S. and Lee, A. (1985) Paired Reading at Colne Valley High School, *Paired Reading Bulletin*, **1**, 46–50.

Cohen, P.A., Kulik, J.A. and Kulik, C–L.C. (1982) Educational outcomes of tutoring: a meta-analysis of findings, *American Educational Research Journal*, **19**(2), 237–48.

* Coldwell, D.C. (1987) A comparative review of five Paired Reading projects at Meltham County Primary School, *Paired Reading Bulletin*, **3**, 6–15.

Cooknell, T. (1985) An inner-city home-reading project, in Topping and Wolfendale (*op. cit.*).

Crombie, R. and Low, A. (1986) Using a Paired Reading technique in cross age peer tutoring, *Paired Reading Bulletin*, **2**, 10–15.

Curtis, M.E. (1980) Development of components of reading skill, *Journal of Educational Psychology*, **72**(5), 656–69.

Dening, T. (1985) A comparison of three parent tutoring methods and the type of post-training support necessary to improve children's reading skills. MSc in Applied Psychology thesis, Murdoch University, Perth, W. Australia.

Diaper, G.R. (1989) A comparative study of Paired Reading techniques using parent, peer and cross-age tutors with second year junior school children PhD thesis. University of Kent.

* Dickinson, D.B. (1986) Paired Reading with children with severe learning difficulties, *Research Exchange (NCSE)*, **6** (September), 2–4.

  * (1987) Paired Reading and children with severe learning difficulties, *Paired Reading Bulletin*, **3**, 28–30.

Downing, J., Schaefer, B. and Ayres, J.D. (1993) *LARR Test of Emergent Literacy*. Windsor: NFER-Nelson.

* Doyle, S. and Lobl, A. (1987) Embedding P.R. in the Curriculum: parent tuition of top infants and cross-age peer tuition in the junior department, *Paired Reading Bulletin*, **3**, 31–9.

* Elliott, J. (1987) Literacy related activities and reading tutoring styles occurring spontaneously in ethnic minority families, *Paired Reading Bulletin*, **3**, 40–4.

  (1989) An investigation of home reading styles: variations in technique and project organisation, *Paired Learning*, **5**, 4–13.

Evans, A. (1984) Paired Reading: a report on two projects. Unpublished paper, Division and Institute of Education, University of Sheffield.

  * (1985) Parental involvement in children's reading: is a structured technique necessary?, *SERCH*, **7**, 11–14.

* Fawcett, B. (1985) The Cowlersely Junior School P.R. project, *Paired Reading Bulletin*, **1**, 42–5.

* Free, L., Harris, C., Martin, J., Morris, S. and Topping, K. (1985) Parent, peer and cross-age tutors, *Paired Reading Bulletin*, **1**, 38–41.

* Gale, I. and Kendall, D. (1985) 'Working Together': the Marsden Junior School Peer Tutor Project, *Paired Reading Bulletin*, **1**, 59–64.

Gautrey, F. (1988) Paired Reading in Reaside Middle School, *Paired Reading Bulletin*, **4**, 12–15 (also in *Reading [UKRA]*, **22**(3), 175–9).

* Gibbs, S. (1988) Reciprocal peer tutored Paired Reading and co-operative learning: a school-based study, MA thesis, University of Nottingham.

* Gillham, B. (1986) Paired Reading in perspective, *Child Education*, **63**(6), 8–9.

Glass, G.V., McGaw, B. and Smith, M.L. (1981) *Meta-analysis in Social Research*, Beverley Hills, CA: Sage.

Gollop, S. (1984) A Paired Reading project in a junior school, *Focus on Language*, **6**, 10–11 (Essex Reading and Language Centre).

Green F, (1987) Analysis of reading tutorial results with an emphasis on consideration of the effectiveness of the Paired Reading procedures. Unpublished paper, Lyndon State College, Lyndonville, Vt., USA.

* Greening, M. and Spenceley, J. (1984) Shared Reading: a review of the Cleveland project, *In-Psych (Bulletin of Cleveland County Psychological Service)*, **11**(2), 10–14.

  * (1985) Shared reading, *Paired Reading Bulletin*, **1**, 20–3.

  * (1987) Shared reading: support for inexperienced readers, *Educational Psychology in Practice*, **3**(1), 31–7.

* Greening, M. and Stephenson, J. (1987) Cleveland reading in secondary schools project – a pilot study, *In-Psych (Bulletin of Cleveland County Psychological Service)*, **12**, 1–8.

  * (1989) CRISP – Cleveland reading in secondary schools project, *Paired Learning*, **5**, 110–17.

Grigg, S. (1984) Parental involvement with reading: an experimental comparison of Paired Reading and listening to children read. MSc (Educational Psychology) dissertation, University of Newcastle-on-Tyne.

Grundy, P. (1987) Parent, teenage volunteer and age peer tutors in the primary school, *Paired Reading Bulletin*, **3**, 45–9.

Hannon, P. (1987) A study of the effects of parental involvement in the teaching of reading on children's reading test performance, *British Journal of Educational Psychology*, **57**(1), 56–72.

Heath, A. (1981) A Paired Reading programme, Edition 2, *I.L.E.A. School Psychological Service*, 22–32.

* (1985) A study of the effectiveness of Paired Reading, in Topping and Wolfendale (*op. cit.*).

Hewison, J. and Tizard, J. (1980) Parental involvement and reading attainment, *British Journal of Educational Psychology*, **50**, 209–15.

* Hodgson, P. (1985) Parental involvement in reading for high school pupils, *Paired Reading Bulletin*, **1**, 14–15.

Holdsworth, P. (1985) Parental involvement at Mowbray School, in Topping and Wolfendale (*op. cit.*).

* (1986) Direct instruction, precision teaching and shared reading, *Paired Reading Bulletin*, **2**, 32–5.

Horowitz, R. and Samuels, S.J. (1985) Reading and listening to expository text, *Journal of Reading Behavior*, **17**(3), 185–98.

Hutson, B.A., Cowger, D.E. and Wallbrown, F.H. (1980) Assessing psycholinguistic orientation and decoding strategies for remedial and non-remedial readers, *Journal of School Psychology*, **18**(3), 263–9.

Johnson, S. (1982) Listening and reading: the recall of 7–9 year olds, *British Journal of Educational Psychology*, **52**, 24–32.

Jones, J.M. (1987) Hawarden infants parent involvement project, *Paired Reading Bulletin*, **3**, 54–61.

* (1988) Paired Reading with mentally handicapped adults: the Ty Pennant pilot project, *Paired Reading Bulletin*, **4**, 78–81.

Joscelyne, T. (1989) Changes in reading style following peer tutored Paired Reading and listening to reading, *Paired Learning*, **5**, 88–93.

(1991) Peer tutored Paired Reading. PhD thesis, University of Sussex.

Jungnitz, G. (1984) A descriptive and comparative study of a parental involvement in reading project with Asian families. MA thesis, University of York.

(1985) A Paired Reading project with Asian families, in Topping and Wolfendale (*op. cit.*).

Jungnitz, G., Olive, S. and Topping, K.J. (1983) The development and evaluation of a Paired Reading project, *Journal of Community Education*, **2**(4), 14–22.

Kidd, A.E. and Levey, M. (1983) Parental involvement in reading in a comprehensive school. Unpublished paper, Birmingham Psychological Service.

Leach, D.J. and Siddall, S.W. (1990) Parental involvement in the teaching of reading: a comparison of Hearing Reading, Paired Reading, Pause Prompt Praise and Direct Instruction Methods, *British Journal of Educational Psychology*, **60**, 349–55.

Lee, A. (1986) A study of the longer term effects of Paired Reading, *Paired Reading Bulletin*, **2**, 36–43.

Lees, E. (1985) An account of a P.R. project, *Paired Reading Bulletin*, **1**, 68–9.

(1986) A cognitive developmental analysis of reading skills in good and poor readers. Paper presented at Annual Conference of Developmental Psychology Section, British Psychological Society, September 1986.

(1987) An analysis of the skills involved in reading development resulting from Paired Reading, *Paired Reading Bulletin*, **3**, 110–12.

Limbrick, E., McNaughton, S. and Glynn T. (1985) Reading gains for underachieving tutors and tutees in a cross-age tutoring programme, *Journal of Child Psychology & Psychiatry*, **26**(6), 939–53.

Lindsay, G. and Evans, A. (1985) Paired Reading and Relaxed Reading: a comparison, *British Journal of Educational Psychology*, **55**(3), 304–9.

Loveday, E. and Simmons, K. (1988) Reading at home: does it matter what parents do?, *Reading (UKRA)*, **22**(2), 84–8.

Low, A. and Davies, M. (1988) Infant/Junior cross-age peer group tuition, *Paired Reading Bulletin*, **4**, 7–10.

Low, A., Madden, L. and Davies, M. (1987) Infant/Junior cross-age peer group tuition, *Paired Reading Bulletin*, **3**, 91–5.

* McKnight, G. (1985) Paired Reading at Lydgate Special School rolls on, *Paired Reading Bulletin*, **1**, 65.

McMillan, G., Young, J., Johnson, J. and Noble, J. (1988) Paired Reading in Edinburgh, in *Innovating Practice* vol. III. Edinburgh: Scottish Education Department/Regional Psychological Services.

Miller, A. (1986) The role of Paired Reading in home-school collaboration schemes, *Curriculum*, **7**(1), 33–8.

(1987) Is there still a place for Paired Reading?, *Educational Psychology in Practice*, **3**(1), 38–43.

* Miller, A., Robson, D. and Bushell, R. (1985) The development of Paired Reading in Derbyshire, in Topping and Wolfendale (*op. cit.*).

(1986) Parental participation in Paired Reading: a controlled study, *Educational Psychology*, **6**(3), 277–84.

Morgan R.T.T. (1976) 'Paired Reading' tuition: a preliminary report on a technique for cases of reading deficit, *Child Care Health and Development*, **2**, 13–28.

* (1985) Paired Reading: origins and future, in Topping and Wolfendale (*op. cit.*).

* (1986) *Helping Children Read: the Paired Reading handbook*. London: Methuen.

* (1986) Paired Reading: history and future, *Paired Reading Bulletin*, **2**, 2–5.

* (1989) Paired Reading: issues and development, in N. Jones (ed.) *Special Educational Needs Review*, vol. 1, London: Falmer Press.

* Morgan, R.T.T. and Bartlett, R. (1988) Parents and pupils learning: Paired Reading in N. Jones (ed.) *Management of Special Needs in Ordinary Schools*. London: Croom Helm.

Morgan R. and Gavin, P. (1988) Paired Reading: evaluation & progress, *Support for Learning*, **3**(4), 201–6.

Morgan, R.T.T. and Lyon, E. (1979) 'Paired Reading' – preliminary report on a technique for parental tuition of reading-retarded children, *Journal of Child Psychology and Psychiatry*, **20**, 151–60.

Morris, A. (1984) A Paired Reading approach – parental involvement at a comprehensive school. Unpublished paper, Division and Institute of Education, University of Sheffield.

Neale, M.D. (1966) *Neale Analysis of Reading Ability* (2nd edn). London: Macmillan.

Neville, M.H. (1968) Effects of oral and echoic responses in beginning reading, *Journal of Educational Psychology*, **59**, 362–9.

(1975) Effectiveness of rate of aural message on reading and listening, *Educational Research*, **18**(1), 37–43.

Newton, M.J., Thomson, M.E. and Richards, I.L. (1979) *Readings in Dyslexia: A Study Text to Accompany the Aston Index*. Wisbech: Learning Development Aids.

O'Hara, M. (1985a) Paired Reading in a school for the physically handicapped, *Paired Reading Bulletin*, **1**, 16–19.

* (1985b) Paired Reading in a social services day nursery, *Paired Reading Bulletin*, **1**, 24–6.

* (1986) Paired Reading with the mentally handicapped, *Paired Reading Bulletin*, **2**, 16–19.

* Oxley, L. (1988) Paired Reading at Cumberworth C. of E. First School, *Paired Reading Bulletin*, **4**, 64–72.

Pitchford, M. and Taylor, P. (1983) Paired Reading, previewing and independent reading. Unpublished paper, Leeds Psychological Service.

* Pitchford, M. (1985) Manipulating the components of Paired Reading, *Paired Reading Bulletin*, **1**, 27–33.

Potter, F. (1982) The use of the linguistic context: do good and poor readers use different strategies? *British Journal of Educational Psychology*, **52**, 16–23.

* Pumfrey, P. (1986) Paired Reading: promise and pitfalls, *Educational Research*, **28**(2), 89–94.

* (1987) A critique of Paired Reading, *Paired Reading Bulletin*, **3**, 62–6.

* Rasinski, T.V. and Fredericks, A.D. (1991) The Akron Paired Reading project, *The Reading Teacher (IRA)*, **44** (7), 514–15.

Richardson, J.R. (1986) Paired Reading in Suffolk, *Paired Reading Bulletin*, **2**, 94.

Ripon, C., Winn, B. and Ingleby, S. (1986) Can parents teach their own children with reading problems?, *Paired Reading Bulletin*, **2**, 76–81.

* Robson, D., Miller, A. and Bushell, R. (1984) The development of Paired Reading in High Peak & West Derbyshire, *Remedial Education*, **19**(4), 177–83.

* Scoble, J., Topping, K.J. and Wigglesworth, C. (1988) Training family and friends as adult literacy tutors, *Journal of Reading (IRA)*, **31**(5), 410–17.

* Scoble, J. (1989) Cued Spelling and Paired Reading in adult literacy, *Paired Learning*, **5**, 57–62.

Scott, J. (1983) Process evaluation of Paired Reading, *Occasional Papers of the Division of Educational & Child Psychology, British Psychological Society*, **7**(1), 82.

Shake, M.C. (1986) Teacher interruptions during oral reading instruction, *Remedial and Special Education*, **7**(5), 18–24.

Simpson, M. (1985) PATCH – parents and teachers with children at home, *Paired Reading Bulletin*, **1**, 66–7.

Smith, D.D. (1979) The improvement of children's oral reading through the use of teacher modelling, *Journal of Learning Disabilities*, **12**(3), 172–5.

Spalding, B., Drew, R., Ellbeck, J., Livesey, J., Musset, M. and Wales, D. (1984) 'If you want to improve your reading, ask your mum', *Remedial Education*, **19**(4), 157–61.

Spiby, G. (1986) A comparative study of the effectiveness of Paired Reading and Reading Aloud among a sample of first year pupils in the remedial department of a comprehensive school. MEd thesis, University College of Swansea.

Sweetlove, M. (1985) Withins School paired Reading project – assessment, Unpublished document, Withins School, Bolton.

(1987) Paired Reading and direct instruction Corrective Reading – comparative and joint effectiveness, *Paired Reading Bulletin*, **3**, 74–82.

* (1988) A cross-age cross-school modular peer tutored Paired Reading course, *Paired Reading Bulletin*, **4**, 43–53.

* Swinson, J.M. (1986) Paired Reading: a critique, *Support for Learning*, **1**(2), 29–32.

Thirkell, B. (1989) Peer tutoring using Paired Reading in a multi-cultural setting, MSc (Educational Psychology) thesis, Polytechnic of East London.

Toepritz, P.I. (1982) A study of parent–child interaction in a Paired Reading project. MSc (Educational Psychology) thesis, University of Sheffield.

* Topping, K.J. (1986a) Effective service delivery: training parents as reading tutors, *School Psychology International*, **7**(4), 231–6.

* (1986b) Paired Reading for adults with literacy problems, *Paired Reading Bulletin*, **2**, 44–52.

* (1986c) WHICH parental involvement in reading scheme?, *Reading (UKRA)* 20(3), 148–56 (also in N. Mercer (ed.) (1988) *Language and Literacy from an Educational Perspective*. Milton Keynes: Open University Press).

* (1987) Correction procedures in parental involvement in reading techniques, *Paired Reading Bulletin*, **3**, 102–108.

* (1987) Paired Reading: a powerful technique for parent use, *The Reading Teacher (IRA)*, **40**(7), 608–14 (also in *Communicacion, Lenguaje y Educacion* (1989), **3–4**, 143–51.)

* (1987) Paired Reading makes a comeback, *Special Children*, **9** (March), 14–15.

* (1987) Peer tutored Paired Reading: outcome data from ten projects, *Educational Psychology*, **7**(2), 133–45 (also in S. Goodlad and B. Hirst (eds) (1990) *Explorations in Peer Tutoring*. Oxford: Blackwell).

* (1988) *Paired Reading Training Pack* (3rd edn). Huddersfield: Kirklees Psychological Service.

* (1988) Peer tutoring of reading using Paired Reading, *Educational and Child Psychology*, **5**(4), 24–8.

* (1989) Parents as reading tutors for children with special needs, in N. Jones (ed.) *Special Educational Needs Review* vol. 1. London: Falmer Press.

* (1989) Peer tutoring and Paired Reading: combining two powerful techniques, *The Reading Teacher* (I.R.A.), **42**(7), 488–94 (also in J.M. Palardy (ed.) (1992) *Introduction to Teaching Reading*, New York: McGraw-Hill).

* (1989) A closer look: Paired Reading, *Child Education*, **66**(6), 13.

* (1989) A whole-school policy on parental involvement in reading, *Reading (UKRA)*, **23**(2), 85–97.

(1990) Outcome evaluation of the Kirklees Paired Reading project. PhD thesis, University of Sheffield.

(1992a) The effectiveness of Paired Reading in ethnic minority homes, *Multicultural Teaching*, **10**(2), 19–23.

(1992b) Short- and long-term follow-up of parental involvement in reading projects, *British Educational Research Journal*, **18**(4), 369–79.

Topping, K.J. and Lindsay, G.A. (1992a) Parental involvement in reading: the influence of socio-economic status and supportive home visiting, *Children and Society (NCB)*, **5**(4), 306–16.

(1992b) The structure and development of the Paired Reading technique, *The Journal of Research in Reading*, **15**(2), 120–36.

(1992c) Paired Reading: a review of the literature, *Research Papers in Education*, **7**(3), 199–246.

* Topping, K.J. and McKnight, G. (1984) Paired Reading – parent power, *Special Education: Forward Trends*, **11**(3), 12–15.

*Topping, K.J. and Scoble, J. (1986) *The Ryedale Adult Literacy Paired Reading Training Pack* (video and paper). Huddersfield: Paired Reading Project, Kirklees Psychological Service.

Topping, K.J. and Shaikh, R. (1989) *Paired Reading in Gujerati, Urdu and English*. Huddersfield: Paired Reading Project, Kirklees Psychological Service (training video).

Topping, K.J. and Whiteley, M. (1990) Participant evaluation of parent-tutored and peer-tutored projects in reading, *Educational Research (NFER)*, **32**(1), 14–32.

(1993) Sex differences in the effectiveness of peer tutoring, *School Psychology International*, **14**(1), 57–67.

Topping, K.J. and Wolfendale, S.W. (eds) (1985) *Parental Involvement in Children's Reading*, London: Croom Helm; New York: Nichols.

* Topping, K.J., Mallinson, A., Gee, A. and Hughes, R. (1985) Paired Reading: a therapeutic technique for maladjusted children, *Maladjustment and Therapeutic Education*, **3**(3), 52–5.

* Townsend, J. and Topping, K.J. (1986) An experiment using P.R. with peer tutors vs. parent tutors, *Paired Reading Bulletin*, **2**, 26–31.

* Townsend, J. (1987) Paired Reading with parent and peer tutors at High Bank First School – an update, *Paired Reading Bulletin*, **3**, 83–4.

* Tyre, C. and Young, P. (1985) Parents as coaches for dyslexic and severely reading-retarded pupils, in Topping and Wolfendale (*op. cit.*).

Ulmer, R. and Green, F. (1988) Parent tutored Paired Reading in a summer program for migrant children, *Paired Reading Bulletin*, **4**, 33–5.

Vaughey, S. and MacDonald, J. (1986) Paired Reading projects with Asian families, *Paired Reading Bulletin*, **2**, 6–9.

Wareing, L. (1983) Comparison of the relative merits of three methods of parental involvement in reading. MSc (Educational Psychology) thesis, North East London Polytechnic.

* (1985) A comparative study of three methods of parental involvement in reading, in Topping and Wolfendale (*op. cit.*).

Welch, S. (1985) An investigation into the use of a P.R. approach by teachers. MSc (Educational Psychology) thesis, North East London Polytechnic.

Welsh, M. and Roffe, M. (1985) Paired Reading projects with Asian families, *Paired Reading Bulletin*, **1**, 34–7.

Wilkinson, A.C. (1980) Children's understanding in reading and listening, *Journal of Educational Psychology*, **72**(4), 561–74.

Winter, S. (1985) Giving parents a choice, in Topping and Wolfendale (*op. cit.*).

(1987) Parents and pupils as remedial tutors, *Bulletin of the Hong Kong Psychologists' Society*, **18**, 15–31.

* (1986) Peers as Paired Reading tutors, *British Journal of Special Education*, **13**(3), 103–6.

(1988) Paired Reading: a study of process and outcome, *Educational Psychology*, **8**,(3), 135–51.

Winter, S. and Low, A. (1984) The Rossmere peer tutor project, *Behavioural Approaches with Children*, **8**(2), 62–5.

* Wisner, M. (1988) Reading while listening, *Paired Reading Bulletin*, **4**, 73–7.

Young, P. and Tyre, C. (1983) *Dyslexia or Illiteracy? Realizing the Right to Read*. Milton Keynes: Open University Press.

Note

The *Paired Reading* and *Paired Learning Bulletins* are available on loan internationally from the Educational Resources Information Centre (ERIC) through any library (microfiche reference numbers: 1985 – ED285124; 1986 – ED285125; 1987 – ED285126; 1988 – ED298429; 1989 – ED313656).

Part Two
Cued Spelling

CHAPTER 6

What Is Cued Spelling?

Spelling is a curriculum area which is neglected and controversial at the same time. Few teachers enjoy teaching spelling and fewer children enjoy learning it. The range of strategies, materials and methods available to teachers is probably smaller and less varied than in any other basic skills area. Yet government and employers keep asserting the importance they attach to spelling. While spelling might not be as important as reading, it is still very important.

Cued Spelling is to spelling what Paired Reading is to reading. So why isn't it called Paired Spelling? Because so many different activities have been passed off under the label of Paired Reading by different practitioners, a more specific name to indicate a specific procedure was thought necessary. So when you see something called Paired Spelling it may, or may not, actually be Cued Spelling as described below.

The design of Cued Spelling deliberately incorporates many of the positive features of Paired Reading. It is a simple and enjoyable technique for one-to-one tutoring by non-professionals on a brief but regular basis. It raises confidence and motivation without needing any special materials or expensive equipment. It is used for parent and peer tutoring and for adult learners with spelling problems.

It also incorporates many of the features of other tried and tested approaches to teaching spelling. It then combines these in a package which is easily and widely used.

Cued Spelling is usually done 3 times per week for an initial 'trial' period of 6 weeks. Each session takes about 15 minutes.

At the outset, Cued Spelling looks rather complicated. Don't be put off. You can train 7-year-olds to do it in half an hour – it's a lot simpler than it looks.

The basic structure of the technique was developed in 1986. It comprises 10 Steps, 4 Points to Remember and 2 Reviews. The structure is illustrated in the Cued Spelling Flowchart. Refer to this as you read on. This flowchart (CSR1) is given to tutors and tutees at the start of training sessions, and may be reproduced for this purpose.

The 10 Steps and 4 Points apply to every individual target word worked upon by the pair, while the 'Speed Review' covers all target words for a particular session and the 'Mastery Review' covers all the target words for one week or a longer period if desired.

The tutee chooses high interest target words irrespective of complexity (Step 1). The pair check the spelling of the word in a dictionary or elsewhere and put a master version in their Cued Spelling Diary (Step 2). (The Cued Spelling Diary (CSR2) is reproduced on p. 75.) They usually also add the word to the top of a piece of paper on which subsequent attempts will be made.

The pair then read the word out loud together (Paired Reading style), then the child reads the word aloud alone (Step 3). This ensures that the tutee is capable of accurate reading and articulation of the word. Without this, spelling attempts are unlikely to succeed!

CSR1   Cued Spelling Flowchart

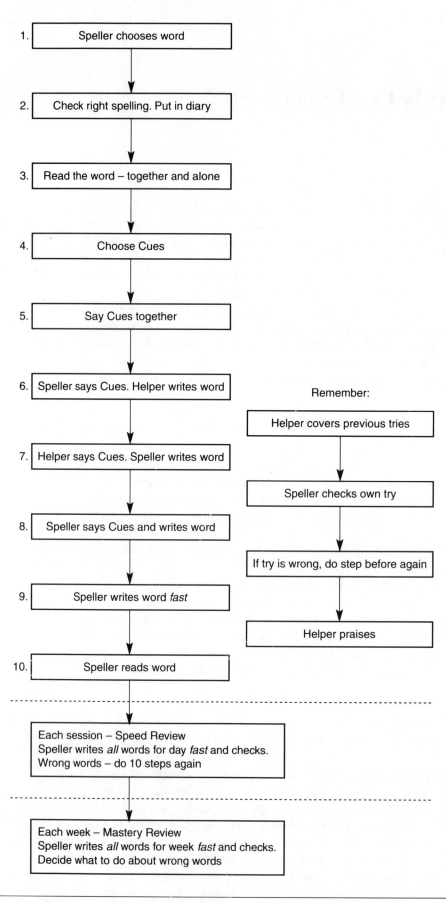

1. | Speller chooses word

2. | Check right spelling. Put in diary

3. | Read the word – together and alone

4. | Choose Cues

5. | Say Cues together

6. | Speller says Cues. Helper writes word

7. | Helper says Cues. Speller writes word

8. | Speller says Cues and writes word

9. | Speller writes word *fast*

10. | Speller reads word

Remember:

Helper covers previous tries

Speller checks own try

If try is wrong, do step before again

Helper praises

Each session – Speed Review
Speller writes *all* words for day *fast* and checks.
Wrong words – do 10 steps again

Each week – Mastery Review
Speller writes *all* words for week *fast* and checks.
Decide what to do about wrong words

Week beginning: ------------			Speed Review Score	Mastery Review Score	Comment or Grade
Monday					
Tuesday					
Wednesday					
Thursday					
Friday					
Saturday					
Sunday					

Professional Comment:

Signed: Date:

The child then chooses Cues (prompts or reminders) to enable him or her to remember the written structure of the word (Step 4). These Cues may be phonic sounds, letter names, syllables or other fragments or 'chunks' of words, or wholly idiosyncratic mnemonic devices.

Tutees are encouraged to consider and choose Cues which fit well with their own cognitive structures, i.e. make sense and are memorable *to them*. Thus, although a tutor might make suggestions or stimulate imagination, the decision on Cueing rests wholly with the tutee.

Once Cues are decided upon, the pair say the Cues out loud simultaneously (Step 5). The tutee then says the Cues out loud while the tutor writes the word down on scrap paper to this 'dictation' (Step 6). Thus the tutee is provided with a demonstration or model of the required behaviour.

Then the tutor says the Cues out loud while the tutee writes down the word (Step 7). The tutee then says the Cues and writes down the word simultaneously (Step 8).

At Step 9, the tutee is required by the tutor to write down the word as fast as possible (the tutee may or may not decide to recite the Cues out loud at this Step, but may well recite them sub-vocally).

At Step 10, the tutee again reads the word out loud as a reminder of the wholeness of the target word and its associated meaning.

The 4 Points cover aspects of the technique relevant to its practical application.

Point 1: At every attempt at writing a target word, the tutor is required to ensure that previous attempts on the work paper are covered up, to avoid the possibility of direct copying. Either the tutor or the tutee might actually effect this.

Point 2: Every time there is a written attempt on a target word, the *tutee* checks the attempt. The tutor only intervenes if the tutee proves unable to check his or her own attempt accurately.

Point 3: If tutees have written a word incorrectly, they are encouraged to cross it out very vigorously to assist its deletion from their memory. At an incorrect attempt, the correction procedure is merely that the pair return to the Step *preceding* the one at which the error was made.

Point 4: Tutors are required to praise tutees regularly and frequently for good performance. In particular, tutors praise for: (a) the tutee putting their own mistake right before checking with the master version, (b) getting each word right at Step 9, (c) getting words right at Reviews (see below). More details of the nature of praise and the criteria for its application are given in training meetings.

At the end of each tutoring session, there is a 'Speed Review'. This means the tutor requires the tutee to write down all the target words for that session, as fast as possible from dictation in random order. The tutee then self-checks all the words with the 'master version' in the Cued Spelling Diary.

Target words which are incorrect at Speed Review have the 10 Steps applied again, perhaps with the choice of different Cues. In fact, tutees make only a small proportion of errors at Speed Review. Thus the requirement to re-apply the 10 Steps is not as onerous as it sounds.

At the end of each week, a 'Mastery Review' is conducted. The tutee is required to write all the target words for the whole week, as fast as possible in random order. The tutee then self-checks all the words with the 'master version' in the Cued Spelling Diary.

No specific error correction procedure is prescribed for Mastery Review. It is left to the pair to negotiate between themselves what they wish to do about errors. Many pairs choose to include failed words in the next week's target words.

A reproducible hand-out for tutors and tutees (CSR3) will be found in Part Four Section B. This describes the method in more detail than the flowchart but more simply than the description above. You might want to look at it now. This hand-out could be given out at the end of a training meeting for future reference.

How Does It Work?

Cued Spelling contains little that is new. It incorporates well-known methods and aspects of accepted 'good practice'. The assembly is more important than the components. It was designed as a coherent package, structured and flexible at the same time.

Cued Spelling is designed to manipulate the surface features of spelling behaviour, just like Paired Reading with reading. It does not presume the existence or possession by the tutee of any spelling 'sub-skills' (whether demonstrated by research or not or whether currently fashionable or not). It is designed to promote the use to maximum effect of whatever skills the tutee does possess. Like Paired Reading, it offers 'positive practice'.

The technique has been designed and structured to be highly interactive, but in operation presents as democratic rather than didactic. It is intended to provide a framework to 'scaffold' self-managed learning.

There is good evidence that spellers naturalistically use a great variety of strategies in a highly idiosyncratic manner, so any *requirement* to use a specific mnemonic strategy all the time is likely merely to further inhibit an already poor speller. Also, there is evidence that when children select their own spelling words, they tend to choose more difficult words, but are as successful as with easier words chosen by adults.

Work on mnemonic strategies has emphasized the importance of meaningfulness to the subject. Thus the Cued Spelling technique fits in well with recent trends towards individualized and self-governed learning of spelling skills.

The technique is 'failure-free', to eliminate student anxiety and promote self-confidence. Swift error correction and support procedures are therefore inbuilt. The technique is also very flexible, useful to tutees of a wide range of age and ability with word sets of infinite variety and complexity.

Tutees are encouraged to self-select interesting and motivating individualized material – some both want and need to master quite specialized vocabulary in the first instance. Additionally, tutees largely control the procedure, deciding themselves about the degree of support they require at any moment.

Modelling is included to give tutees a perfect example of correct performance which they can copy. Being left to work everything out by yourself often results in a high error rate, over-frequent correction and considerable faulty learning.

Praise is essential, for social reinforcement of correct responses but also to promote a tutor behaviour incompatible with damaging criticism. The strong emphasis on understanding is essential for the task to be purposeful for the tutee.

The technique promotes fluency, eliminating stopping and starting and pondering at length about particular words. Thus the steps in the technique are very small incremental stages (i.e. are finely task-analysed). A pair should be able to work through the steps very quickly on easy words, but this should not become boring and frustrating on the longest words. The nature of the activity should ensure high levels of time on task.

Tutees have individual attention and immediate feedback from their tutors, unlikely to be otherwise obtainable. With improved support, motivation and concentration, tutees work on a larger number of words than in more traditional approaches, increasing the amount of practice.

There is a wide gulf between learning to write a word accurately during rote learning or a tutoring session and being able to write it at a different time in a totally different context (e.g. during some creative free writing). The emphasis in the later stages of the technique on speeded performance is drawn from the concept of 'fluency' found in Precision Teaching. This aspect is included to promote generalization over time and contexts, since otherwise there is a danger that the tutee will merely have learned spelling 'tricks' while continuing to spell the same words incorrectly in the course of subsequent continuous free writing.

Lastly, and perhaps most importantly, the technique is clear, straightforward and enjoyable. Both tutor and tutee are easily trained in its use. Neither one of the pair subsequently becomes confused, anxious or bad-tempered about their spelling work together.

You may wish to summarize these advantages in a hand-out for potential participants in a project.

Many of these advantages are in line with research on self-efficacy and motivated learning (e.g. Schunk 1987). Regularity and frequency of success is as important as amount of success. Tutees with difficulties may over-attribute failure to their own inadequacy rather than to deficiencies in teaching. Tutees need to see that success is the result of their own efforts rather than an excess of support or random chance.

Verbalization by the tutee has been shown to facilitate strategic encoding and retention in learning and to promote systematic working. Regularity, frequency and immediacy of feedback are particularly important when tutees are faced with very complex tasks or handicapped by learning disabilities.

Naturally, the method is not just intended to help tutees remember lists of words. As tutees create their own Cues they must think about the auditory, visual, syntactic and semantic structure of the word. It may well be this self-directed interaction rather than the Cue itself which improves retention of the word. With experience and by making connections with taught spelling knowledge, tutees more readily perceive consistencies in word structures.

Cued Spelling thus provides a framework within which the tutee can 'make sense of spelling' – but make their *own* sense of it. Spelling is of course conceptual as well as perceptual, and tutees need to form predictive concepts about how words work. As the interactive procedures of Cued Spelling involve them in comparing and contrasting, they may organize and integrate these concepts for themselves more effectively.

Teachers sometimes have worries about the Cued Spelling method before trying it out. They might wonder if the method promotes 'mere memorization' or supports spelling exclusively by 'Cues'. In practice, the tutees end up remembering the words but not usually the Cues. As they become more used to the method, their Cues become more systematic and reflective of the regularities in our language as well as their own favoured learning style. Their powers of prediction of regularities in new words are certainly increased. The evaluation results showing generalization of improved spelling capability to the completely new words in norm-referenced spelling tests are a clear indication of that.

Where Does It Fit?

There is less than full agreement about how specific spelling instruction should be integrated within the curriculum. Is good spelling 'caught' or does it have to be taught? From a visual orientation, work on word patterns and word clusters is often popular – but the skills may not be retained and generalized to free writing. For other teachers, phonic strategies are the main method of choice – yet less than half of the words in the English language are phonically regular. With older children, spelling rules come more into play – but the complexity of our language means a vast number of rules and exceptions need to be remembered and applied.

Many teachers will be familiar with the 'Look-Cover-Write-Check' method to help remember spellings. This has the advantages of being quick, cheap and self-managed by children. Unfortunately the method also has the disadvantage of being primarily visually oriented. By itself, it might be suitable and effective for some words and some children. But only some. Thus you will find elements of 'Look-Cover-Write-Check' within the Cued Spelling package – but Cued Spelling goes further, offers more options and individual flexibility, and should be effective with many more words and many more children.

Just as with learning to read, there are many different pathways to becoming a competent speller. Turner and Quinn (1986) found that younger children tended to rely on auditory information irrespective of the nature of the word, while for older children visual information produced better results. They concluded: 'the learner must draw on several strategies . . . no single strategy can be used to overcome all irregularities in written English'.

As with reading, over-teaching in any specific narrow instructional channel can do more harm than good – particularly where the type of instruction does not correspond to the tutee's strongest sensory modality and/or learning style. Teachers still sometimes try to teach all children to spell in the way they themselves spell successfully. But of course this is not the best way for all (or perhaps even many) of the children. However, most teachers have no time to analyse the individual spelling profile of every child in the class and prescribe and manage a wide range of individual spelling programmes.

One solution is to help children to manage their own learning. As one of the strands in your spelling instruction programme you can adopt methods which free the children to follow their own favoured pathways, yet within a strongly supportive general framework. You can do this in an interactive way which involves the children in evaluating for themselves the success of their own strategies. This is what Cued Spelling is all about.

Cued Spelling is different from, but complementary to, regular teacher-directed classroom instruction in spelling. The method is set in the context of research and thinking on spelling.

Teaching styles which encourage children to work out the learning strategies which are most effective for themselves are increasingly favoured (e.g. Pressley 1990, Scheid 1993). Scruggs and his co-workers have carried out a series of experiments on 'mnemonic strategies' (e.g. Scruggs and Laufenberg 1986) which show the importance of enhancing recall by representations meaningful *to the individual*.

These workers found such strategies more effective in terms of immediate and delayed recall of spellings than a direct instruction spelling programme (Veit *et al.* 1986). In a similar vein, Wong (1986) developed a successful self-monitoring strategy for children, while emphasizing that they also needed to be taught specific information about words.

Coupled with these trends is the growth in organizing teaching and learning in cooperative, interactive ways (e.g. Topping 1988, Slavin 1990). However, this is not easy in the area of spelling, which is still sometimes taught in a very old-fashioned way even in classrooms where the rest of the curriculum is delivered very differently.

Intensive rote learning of high-frequency, commonly misspelt words is much less in favour than previously. Much more prominence is currently given to relating instruction to developmental stages in children's spelling errors, identifying existing levels of knowledge and building instructional sequences controlling the increasing complexity of the task (Read 1975, Henderson and Beers 1980, Gentry 1982, Cummings 1988, Henderson 1990, Templeton and Bear 1992).

Various spelling error analysis methods have been devised to help teachers in this regard (e.g. Gable *et al.* 1988, Schlagel 1989, Hepburn 1991). However, hard-pressed teachers sometimes resort to the highly notional 'developmental sequences' found in basal spelling series. In any case, overall developmental tendencies do not relate directly to each individual spelling by each individual child.

This has led to approaches designed to extend children's transferable spelling skills via learning to spell words chosen by the tutee as of high interest as well as utility. Research suggests that where children select their own spelling words, the self-selected words are usually longer and more complex than those chosen by the teacher, but are retained to at least the same degree (e.g. Michael 1986). Similarly, Gettinger (1985) found that children with specific spelling problems made better progress when they were actively involved in a learning strategy than when similar routines were imposed by teachers.

In the UK, Moseley (1987) reported another teaching approach involving tutee self-selection of spelling words. He noted that many existing spelling programmes suffered from three main weaknesses: (a) a lack of generalization of skills from mere study of spelling patterns, (b) introduction of skills in teaching sequences based on opinion and 'average' developmental sequences rather than analyses of children's actual errors, and (c) a lack of flexibility, so tutees found little interest or relevance in the tasks presented. Individualized self-managed learning of spelling skills could help to resolve these problems.

Cued Spelling is not intended to replace other methods available to the teacher. Computer Aided Learning, tactile and kinaesthetic methods and special phonic dictionaries can happily be used in conjunction with Cued Spelling, or as an alternative to provide variety and promote generalization. This is also true of expensive audio-visual approaches such as 'ARROW', as well as various commercial spelling schemes published for classroom use.

Adaptations

The Cued Spelling procedure described above has been used successfully with tutees as young as 7 years. More able and mature children chronologically even younger than this may be able to use the technique. However, adaptation for use with younger and less able children might be indicated.

A suggested abbreviated Cued Spelling procedure for this purpose will be found in Part Four Section B (CSR6). You might wish to try this out. Remember that it has not been evaluated like the full Cued Spelling procedure.

CHAPTER 7

How to Organize and Evaluate Cued Spelling

Cued Spelling projects follow many of the organizational guidelines for Paired Reading projects. You will be able to use much of the Paired Reading parent and peer-tutoring planning proformas. The Context and Objectives sections will still apply. Very similar organizational questions must be answered about Recruitment, Selection and Matching, Training, Organization of Contact, Support and Monitoring, Feedback and Evaluation. One planning area which is very different is, of course, Materials. In what follows repetition will be avoided as far as possible, emphasis being given to significant organizational difference for Cued Spelling as compared to Paired Reading.

Context and Objectives should be considered and specified much as for Paired Reading. This is also true of Recruitment.

Selection and Matching

Potential Cued Spellers should be able to read a bit, know the names and sounds of at least some letters and be able to write legibly. Those who can't write might still be able to do Cued Spelling by using a typewriter or computer, letter cards or plastic letters.

As with Paired Reading, you will wish to consider how many in a class you can effectively support and monitor at one time. You may wish to start with a few volunteers in the first instance. Others in the class can do other kinds of spelling work – and give you interesting possibilities of evaluative comparison. As with Paired Reading, you do need a group of sufficient size and variety to offer mutual support and not feel stigmatized or 'picked on'.

Tutors do not necessarily have to be better spellers than tutees. If they are about as good (or bad!) as each other, they need to take special care to look up every word carefully in the dictionary or other master source. They also need to be very careful to copy the master version into Cued Spelling Diaries very accurately. Otherwise there is a great danger of the pair overlearning incorrect spellings. Cued Spelling is a powerful procedure – if you don't start off right, you will spell the word wrong forever!

This possibility of same-ability pairing does open up interesting possibilities. A parent who is of limited spelling ability could work with their child of similar spelling ability, or sibling tutoring could operate between children of similar or different ages. Particularly in peer tutoring, you may wish to opt for reciprocal tutoring – where the roles of tutor and tutee swap round at predetermined intervals. Roles can reciprocate after each session or after each week.

There are many advantages to reciprocal tutoring. Everybody gets to be a tutor during the project, so nobody feels inferior. Everybody knows the role of both tutor and tutee, so rematching pairs when covering for absences is much easier. The variety helps stave off boredom.

Of course, both members of the pair end up learning their own and their partner's words. This could be tested by having the tutees give terminal total Mastery Reviews on the tutee's words to the tutors, rather than the other way round.

For peer-tutoring matching purposes, draw up a ranked list of more to less able spellers from spelling test results or class observation. If you opt for cross-ability fixed role tutoring, draw a line through the middle of the list to separate tutors from tutees. Then match the most able tutor to the most able tutee, and so on down the list to maintain roughly the same differential in spelling ability in each pair.

However, if you opt for same-ability (and probably reciprocal role) tutoring, do not divide the ranked list. Just match first with second, third with fourth, and so on. You will see that one disadvantage of same-ability tutoring is that the two weakest spellers in the class will be working together. This is acceptable so long as they are not also the most disorganized and distractable. You will need to monitor them closely in any case – but don't you always?

As with Paired Reading, do not worry unduly about cross-gender matching, but do try to keep blatantly non-compatible personalities apart. Consider appointing spare tutors.

Materials

Participant pairs need a pen or pencil, scrap paper, a piece of card, an appropriate dictionary, a Cued Spelling Flowchart, a Cued Spelling Diary and a Cued Spelling Collecting Book. The flowchart and diary are easily reproduced (see Chapter 6, CSR1 and 2) and the collecting book is just a little rough notebook with blank pages. Little time or cost is involved.

Dictionaries can be more problematic. Some schools do not have enough in class for each pair to have their own. Some families will not have one at home and a loan from school may have to be explored. The nature of the dictionary is also an issue. In a regular mixed-ability class there is usually only one standard dictionary issued. This will be too hard for the weaker pairs to access and not contain the difficult words the more able pairs wish to work on. A range of dictionaries is needed.

Remember that for Cued Spelling it is assumed that the tutees know the meaning of the words they choose. Definitional dictionaries are not needed for this purpose. Schools may wish to invest in a number of small cheap spelling dictionaries which only give correct spellings. These are often particularly good at including strange plurals and declensions with which spellers have trouble.

Training

Training tutors and tutees together is usual and least consuming of time. (However, some schools have trained children first and then parents later.) Ensure that trainees have pen or pencil, scrap paper, piece of card, appropriate dictionary and sample page from spelling diary. The tutees must have 'collected' five words they want to learn how to spell better and brought these to the training meeting for practice purposes.

Be welcoming – establishing an informal, friendly, communicating atmosphere is essential. In an introduction briefly set the national and local Cued Spelling scene and mention positive evaluation results. Briefly highlight the differences between Cued Spelling and more traditional approaches: (a) use of high interest, specialist, hard words, (b) use of any friendly tutor, and (c) brief but regular and frequent commitment. Emphasize that it may be fun but it will still be real work.

Distribute 10 Steps Flowcharts, one per pair, at the start of the meeting. (If you are using the abbreviated procedure, substitute copies of CSR6.) Say that Cued Spelling has 10 Steps, 4 Points to Remember and 2 Reviews. Emphasize that although it seems complicated, it's really quite easy. You might wish to give a quick demonstration of a pair going through the 10 Steps on a word (taking little over 2 minutes), to reinforce this.

Then talk about what the 10 Steps are. Refer to the Cued Spelling Flowchart all the time. You might wish to also display this enlarged on an overhead projector. Demonstrate the Steps live or on video. A live demonstration of Cued Spelling often lacks clarity of small detail and tends to be less successful. A fast demonstration then a slow one with pauses for commentary might prove most effective.

When you come to Step 4 'Choosing Cues', take time to elaborate on what this means. Mention alphabetic/phonic/syllabic/mnemonic options. Give an example of each. You will need to use a chalkboard or write on overhead transparencies to show what you mean. Solicit examples of 'hard words to spell' from the tutees. Solicit suggestions from the group for different Cues for these. Strongly emphasize that different people will use different Cues. There is no such thing as the 'right' Cue, only the Cue which is best (i.e. most effective) for the individual. However, you may wish to relate Cueing to recent classroom instruction in spelling.

Similarly, then give a talk on the 4 points and each of the 2 Reviews. You will want to demonstrate each of these live or on video also, while referring to the flowchart.

Then have the pairs go off to practise. They will need tables and chairs for this. Access to the required materials should be indicated. You might wish to display suggested 'practice' words for those who have arrived without their own. Likewise, arrange substitute tutees/tutors or role play if some 'pairs' are incomplete.

Experienced Cued Spellers should then circulate and check practice. There should be a monitor/trainee ratio sufficient to ensure a minimum of 3 minutes individual attention for each pair during practice. As with Paired Reading, use a three-step remediation sequence for those needing further coaching: (1) praise good practice and point out faulty aspects, giving further verbal advice, (2) join in with pair and proceed as a triad, and (3) take over from the tutor and redemonstrate with the tutee.

On return to the large group, the trainer can comment generally on practice observed and solicit questions from group. Then brief the group about organizational issues, e.g. time commitment, where to 'collect' words from, where to keep collected words (some projects give out a rough collecting book), how to keep records in the Cued Spelling Diary, when and how to have records verified and responded to by the teacher, and so on. Tutees should show their Cued Spelling Diaries to the class teacher once each week.

Emphasize that the children are encouraged to choose words from their school spelling books, graded free writing, relevant project work, special Cued Spelling displays of common problem words or groups of words selected as developmentally appropriate by the teacher. Tutees should collect these (in a Cued Spelling 'collecting book'), so they always have a pool of suitable words from which to choose.

Distribute materials required: complete Cued Spelling Diary, collecting books and hand outs with further ideas on Cueing and mnemonics (CSR4 and 5 in Part Four Section B). Describe support, trouble-shooting and feedback arrangements, much as with Paired Reading. In Cued Spelling Diaries, each page includes space to write the master version of up to 10 words on all days of the week, together with boxes to record daily Speed Review and weekly Mastery Review scores and spaces for comments from tutor (daily) and teacher (weekly) (see CSR2 in Chapter 6).

Specify the initial contract, namely a minimum of 5 words per day for 3 days per week (time about 15 minutes per session) for 6 weeks. Secure verbal or written commitment from the participants. Participating children might receive a badge.

Allow 1 hour 15 minutes for the whole meeting, assuming a punctual start and excluding refreshment and general discussion time.

Contact

Organization of contact is much the same as for peer-tutored Paired Reading. Try to keep the 3 sessions per week well spaced to counteract boredom. Schedule 15 minutes per session and expect 5 words and Speed Review to be completed in this time. If pairs choose to go on longer in their own time, they can proceed at a more leisurely pace.

Remember chairs and tables will be needed and some noise will result. The demands on space will be significant. Children like to spread over into other spaces for extra privacy.

Support and Monitoring

Advice in Chapter 3 applies here also. In a peer-tutoring project you will find the children readily ask for help with difficult words. Make sure you give them only correct spellings – many teachers are more sure about their own spelling capabilities than they have cause to be! Encourage checking with the dictionary.

As you observe pairs in action, check that there are four correct written attempts for every word on their scrap paper. If you cannot see at least four attempts, the pair are missing out some Steps.

Check the pair's organization of the necessary materials – too much clutter on the table can result in much fussing and time spent off task. Ensure that mistakes are corrected as the method prescribes and generosity (or slackness) does not creep in. Some tutors are just too helpful and do too much for their tutee, risking creating dependence and learned helplessness. Encourage an emphasis on speed and high rates of time on task. Keep an eye out for social friction in the pair.

Vet any creative adaptations a pair start making to the method very carefully for effectiveness and mutual acceptability.

Also keep a watch on the words chosen, since some tutees might choose words they already know, while others may choose some extremely difficult words of very doubtful long-term utility. Neither will do much to help the development of generalized understanding about the structure of words. A very simple initial rule can be 'three for everyday use and two just for fun'.

Watch out for pairs who have locked into narrow themes (e.g. football) and are overlearning too much specialist vocabulary. The children may need reminding that the whole point of the exercise is to help them spell better in the course of everyday free writing. Being able to perform a few exotic but otherwise useless spelling 'tricks' is not what it's about. Also beware of pairs who like to create baroque mnemonics as an art form in itself, irrespective of any value in improving spelling.

Tutees tend to voice two main difficulties. One is finding words and the other is finding Cues. Promoting the 'collection' of words is important. Should the (cautious) teacher have chosen to set a ceiling of difficulty on words chosen, the most competent pairs may soon feel they can spell everything below that ceiling and frustration can set in.

All pairs will have difficulty finding interesting Cues for some words. Occasional whole-class sessions on Cueing can be held, for brainstorming good Cues for such words, elaborating different approaches (see CSR4 and 5) and linking Cueing to spelling instruction in school. Encourage comparing and contrasting to help children perceive, relate and map spelling regularities. You might like to establish a display board for favourite mnemonics and praise words (which the children might like to illustrate).

Partners can be swopped at a later stage to increase novelty and widen the social effects of the tutoring.

Remember Cued Spelling makes you more of a teacher – a co-ordinator of effective learning experiences in and out of school. The organization of a project, running a training session and carefully monitoring the activities involved all demand sophisticated professional skills.

Also remember Cued Spelling can save you time. Close teacher observation during peer-tutored Cued Spelling can prove invaluable for assessment purposes.

Feedback

At the feedback meeting after the 6 weeks intensive trial period, you will wish to explore pairs' views on continuation options. As with Paired Reading, if in doubt keep them hungry.

Evaluation

As with all evaluation, this should be conducted with reference to the objectives set for the project, which may be academic, affective, social or a combination of these. A number of the research designs and evaluative methods described in Chapter 5 for Paired Reading apply here also, e.g. verbal evaluative feedback from consumers in individual and group meetings.

Cued Spelling does of course have its own evaluation system in-built in the form of Mastery Reviews. You may wish to aggregate the scores from weekly Mastery Reviews. These are readily obtainable from the Cued Spelling Diaries.

Many project co-ordinators also conduct total Mastery Reviews at the end of the intensive period as a check on longer term retention. Some children will have worked on a very large number of words and you may need to stagger these 'Mega-Mastery Reviews' in sections, otherwise the children will be overwhelmed. You should anticipate an average score of 80 per cent correct on this overall Review if the project has worked satisfactorily. A longer-term follow-up some weeks after the intensive period would be a valuable check on retention.

Cued Spelling does of course seek to do more than help children remember a number of difficult words. It also aims to improve general spelling skills. Therefore, evaluation efforts should in addition examine the generalization of improved spelling skills – to new words never the subject of Cued Spelling activity, and to new contexts outside the framework of Cued Spelling, e.g. continuous free writing.

A number of standardized (norm-referenced) spelling tests have been used to evaluate the generalization of Cued Spelling gains to completely new words. This can be related to 'normal' expectations or (preferably) to a control group. In fixed-role tutoring, the gains of the tutors as well as those of the tutees can be assessed and compared. In reciprocal role tutoring, everyone will have been both tutor and tutee, so this comparison will not be possible.

Standardized tests used to date for this purpose in the UK include the Daniels and Diack Graded Spelling Test, the Vincent and Claydon Diagnostic Spelling Test, the Vernon Graded Word Spelling Test and Young's SPAR Test (see references). Alternatively, criterion-referenced tests could be applied on a before and after basis, perhaps drawn from lists of high-frequency words in writing or from lists of frequently misspelt words.

Some spelling tests (e.g. the Vincent and Claydon) include measures of 'self-esteem as a speller' and these may give some indication of attitude to self, possibly comparing before and after project scores and contrasting with a non-participant group if possible.

Attitudinal gains may also be found with respect to liking spelling itself, liking other related curricular areas, liking peer tutoring *per se* irrespective of content, and so on. Social gains might be explored via questionnaire, sociometry or observation. You may wish to see whether the project has resulted in greater social interaction outside tutoring sessions across genders, social classes, ethnic groupings, age groups, ability groups, and so on.

Reproducible sample subjective Feedback Questionnaires for tutors and tutees will be found in Part Four Section B (CSR7). These offer a quick and easy way of obtaining consumer feedback which is readily summarized.

Attempts to analyse free writing for better spelling are problematic. Just as with Paired Reading, if a simple error count is used on a before and after basis, this takes no account of tutees becoming more ambitious. If post-project they are reading harder books or trying to spell harder words, they may make as many errors as before, but at a higher level.

Some sort of allowance for difficulty might be considered, perhaps involving before and after comparison of error rate in bands of two-syllable words, three-syllable words, four-syllable words, and so on. This would offer only the crudest of indices, however. There is certainly scope for creative invention in the evaluation of the impact of Cued Spelling – or indeed any other spelling intervention.

CHAPTER 8

Does Cued Spelling Work?

The initial reports on Cued Spelling were of a descriptive nature, but nonetheless fascinating. Emerson (1988) reported on a brief project using the technique with four parents who tutored their own children at home. Results at Mastery Review were excellent.

Scoble (1988) reported a detailed case study of an Adult Literacy student tutored by his wife using the technique. After 10 weeks of Cued Spelling, a Mastery Review of all words covered in the preceding weeks yielded a success rate of 78 per cent.

Subsequently, Scoble (1989) reported on the progress of fourteen similar pairs, most of whom had done Paired Reading together first. The most long-standing student had used the method for over a year and usually achieved Speed Review scores of 100 per cent and Mastery Review scores of 90 per cent. Harrison (1989) reported on a similar project and its extension to peer tutoring between Adult Literacy students in an evening-class situation.

In the event, however, the most popular application of Cued Spelling then proved to be in a peer-tutoring format. Oxley and Topping (1990) reported on a project in which eight seven- and eight-year-old pupils were tutored by eight nine-year-old pupils in the same vertically grouped class in a small rural school.

This cross-age, cross-ability, fixed-role, peer-tutoring project was found to yield striking social benefits. The children became more cooperative and self organizing as a group. Cross-age friendships became much more prevalent. They spontaneously praised each other in many different situations. Without any staff involvement, two tutors initiated a 'Friendly Patrol' in the playground at break (recess) time, distributing stickers for positive social performances, such as being 'smiley'. They also spontaneously generalized peer tutoring to other curricular areas, such as instrumental music and mathematics, and to other situations, such as with siblings at home.

Subjective feedback from both tutors and tutees was very positive (see CSR7 in Part Four Section B). In eight tutorial pairs, all the tutors and all but two tutees found Cued Spelling easy to learn to do. Two tutees found it hard to think of good words and three found it hard to think of good Cues. All eight tutees reported they now felt happier about spelling and now did better at spelling tests. All but one felt they self-corrected more. However, few reported perceiving an improvement in their spelling in the course of free writing. All the tutees said they enjoyed Cued Spelling but only five of the tutors said this. Five tutees wished to continue with Cued Spelling but none of the tutors wished to do so.

The self-concept as a speller of both tutees and tutors showed a marked positive shift compared to that of non-participant children, and especially so for the tutees. (This was measured using the Vincent-Claydon Self Concept as a Speller Scale.)

After 6 weeks, a total Mastery Review of all target words yielded average scores of 66 per cent correct, with great variability between pairs, but a test session of up to 92 items for such young children was considered of doubtful reliability. Also, some of the tutees had chosen many words of great difficulty and doubtful utility.

Results on two norm-referenced tests of spelling (Vincent-Claydon and SPAR) were equivocal. The SPAR Test suffered from a ceiling effect with some tutors and the Vincent-Claydon from a 'floor effect' with the weakest tutees. On the SPAR Test, tutees made ratio gains of 2.26 and tutors made ratio gains of 2.78. However, although the scores of both tutees and tutors were strikingly improved at post-test, so were those of non-participant children in the same class.

This may be attributed to practice effects on the test (although parallel forms were used), to the 'John Henry Effect', to contamination between groups, or some combination of factors. This study does demonstrate the importance of having control or comparison groups, however. The correlation between results on the two standardized tests and between those and Mastery Review scores was not high. This perhaps illustrates the desirability of evaluation by 'multiple measures of independent imperfection'.

Peer-tutored Cued Spelling on a larger scale in a class-wide, same-age, same-ability reciprocal tutoring format was reported by Brierley *et al.* (1989). All pupils in the three first-year, mixed-ability classes (aged 9 to 10 years) in a Middle School participated. Tutor and tutee roles changed each week. All 75 children were trained in a single group meeting and practised back in their own classes. This is very economical of time but not necessarily recommended!

After 6 weeks, a total Mastery Review of all words covered yielded average scores of 80 per cent correct. The highest number of correct spellings at final Mastery Review was 54 and the highest percentage success rate 100 per cent. There are problems in expressing Mastery Review scores in summary form, since neither percentage correct nor number correct gives an adequate overview of performance in a situation where different children were attempting different numbers of target words of varying difficulty with various levels of success. Given this, and other factors, the correlation between Mastery Review scores and norm-referenced test scores may not be high or particularly meaningful. In this study, that correlation was low.

On a norm-referenced test of spelling (Daniels and Diack Graded Spelling Test), the average gain for all children was 0.65 years of spelling age during the six-week project, certainly many times more than normal expectations, despite the ceiling effect of this test artificially depressing the results. The average for one class was 0.47 years gain, that for another 0.7 years. The best individual gain in Spelling Age was 2.1 years.

Subjective feedback from the children was very positive, 90 per cent of children feeling that Cued Spelling was easy to learn to do. Eighty-four per cent reported feeling happier about spelling in general, 69 per cent of the children said they were better at spelling tests after the project and 65 per cent said their spelling in free writing was better. Eighty-five per cent felt their self-correction had improved. Two-thirds said they liked Cued Spelling. However, only 53 per cent of the children reported finding it easy to think of good Cues and only 38 per cent found it easy to think of good target words.

There were striking differences between classes in subjective feedback, including wishes for continuation. In the 'most enthusiastic' class, 39 per cent of the children wished to do Cued Spelling five times a week, another 39 per cent wished to do it twice a week, and 22 per cent wished to carry on with spelling work but in a different way. Across all three classes, however, the average proportion wishing to carry on doing Cued Spelling was 47 per cent. This clearly demonstrates that even with identical initial input, what the co-ordinating teacher does subsequently in the classroom can make a big difference. However, even the results from the 'least enthusiastic' class were pretty good.

Subsequently, peer-tutored Cued Spelling was initiated by a number of schools, especially in the reciprocal tutoring format, but few found time to evaluate it.

A study of parent-tutored Cued Spelling with 47 children of 8 years of age and of the normal range of spelling ability was undertaken by France *et al.* (1993). This school already had a whole-school policy on spelling, all teachers promoted the Look-Cover-Write-Check method and carried out considerable classwork on phoneme and morpheme clusters, as well as operating 'sponsored spells' and other related events.

The results indicated that the intervention appeared to be effective in differentially raising the spelling attainments of participants as compared to non-participants, at least in the short term. A participant sample of 22 children and a non-participant comparison group of 10 children in the same class were tested (Daniels and Diack Graded Spelling Test). The Cued Spellers on average gained 0.51 years of spelling age in 6 weeks while the comparison group gained 0.18 years. (The comparison group tended to be slightly more able spellers at pretest.) Female Cued Spellers did especially well according to the test results.

Children felt Cued Spelling was easy to learn to do and that it improved their spelling along a number of dimensions. Sixty-nine per cent reported improved performance on spelling tests and in self correction, while 74 per cent reported improved spelling in continuous free writing. Fully 85 per cent said they were happier about spelling. Sixty-nine per cent reported it was easy to find Cues but 77 per cent found it hard to find good words. However, 62 per cent said they tended to become bored with it. Nevertheless, 72 per cent said they wanted to go on doing it!

Despite the emphasis on 'collecting' words, parents reported children had not always managed to do this. Other children deliberately chose very hard words and built in failure for themselves, despite being counselled about this. Some children applied phonic Cues to constructions which sounded the same yet had different meanings, to the discomfiture of the parent tutor. Generally, however, the parents approved of and appreciated the project.

It can be argued that any method involving extra time on task at spelling and extra valuable parental attention and approval related to spelling might be likely to yield differential gains. A study by Watt and Topping (1993) compared Cued Spelling with traditional spelling homework (an alternative intervention involving equal tutor attention and equal time on spelling tasks), and compared the relative effectiveness of parent and peer-tutored Cued Spelling and assessed the generalization of the effect of Cued Spelling into subsequent continuous free writing.

On a norm-referenced spelling test, the 23 Cued Spellers gained over 2 months of spelling age on the Vernon Spelling Test for each chronological month elapsed, and a sub-sample showed even larger gains on the Blackwell Spelling Workshop Test, while the traditional spelling homework comparison group of more able spellers gained only half a month of spelling age per month. Parent and peer tutoring seemed equally effective.

The average score for parent-tutored children at final Mastery Review of words used in the programme was 93 per cent correct. The Mastery Reviews were staggered rather than completed at one sitting. Parent and peer tutoring seemed equally effective.

Participating children returned questionnaires identical to those used by Oxley and Topping (1990). Of these, 56 per cent found it easy to think up good Cues while the rest thought it hard, but 87 per cent now felt happier about spelling in general and that their spelling was better when writing, while 83 per cent felt they now did better at spelling tests. Ninety-one per cent reported a higher rate of self-correction after doing Cued Spelling and the same proportion said they liked doing Cued Spelling, while 87 per cent said they wished to go on doing Cued Spelling.

Parents returned feedback questionnaires and 88 per cent reported a higher rate of self-correction, confirming the feedback from the children, while 58 per cent reported noticing their children spontaneously generalize the use of Cued Spelling techniques to other words. Three of the four teachers involved noted higher rates of self-correction of spelling in classwork and a general improvement in free writing.

Pre–post analysis of written work was based on samples of writing from eighteen Cued Spellers and a small number of comparison children. Cued Spellers tended to produce longer pieces of writing after the project compared to before it, and in all but one case the proportional number of misspellings had reduced, despite evidence of inclusion of more ambitious and exotic vocabulary. The comparison group also tended to produce longer pieces at post-test but error rate did not show the same decrease. The average number of spelling errors per page reduced from 8.5 to 4.62 for the Cued Spellers and from 3.7 to 2.1 for the comparison children, who clearly had a lower error rate to start with and thus had less room for improvement.

Generally, all but one of the participants and all but one of the comparison children were adjudged to have improved in quality of written work (one would of course expect children in school to improve over time), but the Cued Spelling group recorded an average of 1.7 specific improvements per child while the comparison group averaged 1.25. Analysis was based on these categories: Detail of language and semantics, Vocabulary, Structure and planning, Spelling, Punctuation, Repetition and redundancy, Complexity of grammar and Accuracy of grammar.

This study appears to have shown the superiority of Cued Spelling over traditional spelling homework and weekly spelling tests.

Summary

The research on Cued Spelling is much less voluminous than that on Paired Reading. Cued Spelling is, of course, much newer than Paired Reading, but also focuses on a less vital skill. Although the Cued Spelling research has included control or comparison groups and has checked generalization of gains into other contexts, there is as yet no longer-term follow-up evidence. Studies to assess whether Cued Spelling gains 'wash out' in the long run are needed.

Nevertheless, the picture to date is very positive. Cued Spelling seems to improve self-esteem. Both parent and peer-tutored Cued Spelling has led to an average ratio gain on standardized spelling tests of 4.1 times normal expectations (range 2.2 to 5.0). Mastery Review at project end shows average retention of 82 per cent of target words (range 66 per cent to 93 per cent).

The vast majority of children find Cued Spelling easy to learn to do. After Cued Spelling, a large majority report that they feel happier about spelling (84 per cent – 100 per cent) and are better at self correcting (69 per cent – 91 per cent) and spelling tests (69 per cent – 100 per cent). A smaller majority report perceiving generalized improvement in spelling in free writing (average 68 per cent, range 24 per cent – 87 per cent). Most children say they wish to carry on doing Cued Spelling (range 47 per cent to 87 per cent).

Difficulties encountered by some children are finding 'good' target words (range 25 per cent – 77 per cent) and thinking up good Cues (range 31 per cent – 47 per cent). This clearly highlights the need for Cued Spelling projects to give special emphasis to these organizational aspects.

References

Brierley, M., Hutchinson, P., Topping, K. and Walker, C. (1989) Reciprocal peer tutored Cued Spelling with ten year olds, *Paired Learning*, **5**, 136–40.

Cummings, D. (1988) *American English Spelling*. Baltimore, Md.: John Hopkins University Press.

Daniels, J.C. and Diack, H. (1979) *The Standard Reading Tests*. St Albans, Hertfordshire: Hart-Davis Educational.

Emerson, P. (1988) Parent Tutored Cued Spelling in a primary school, *Paired Reading Bulletin*, **4**, 91–2.

Formentin, T. and Csapo, M. (1980) *Precision Teaching*. Vancouver: Centre for Human Development and Research.

France, L., Topping, K. and Revell, K. (1993) Parent tutored Cued Spelling, *Support for Learning*, **8**(1), 11–15.

Gable, R.A., Hendrickson, J.M. and Meeks, J.W. (1988) Assessing spelling errors of special needs students, *The Reading Teacher (IRA)*, **41**(3), 112–17.

Gentry, R. (1982) An analysis of developmental spelling in GYNS at work, *The Reading Teacher (IRA)*, **36**(3), 192–200.

Gettinger, M. (1985) Effects of teacher-directed versus student-directed instruction and cues versus no cues for improving spelling, *Journal of Applied Behavior Analysis*, **18**, 167–71.

Harrison, R. (1989) Cued Spelling in adult literacy in Kirklees, *Paired Learning*, **5**, 141.

Henderson, E. (1990) *Teaching Spelling*, Boston. Houghton Mifflin.

Henderson, E. and Beers, J. (eds) (1980) *Developmental and Cognitive Aspects of Learning to Spell: a reflection of word knowledge*, Newark. DE: International Reading Association.

Hepburn, J. (1991) Spelling categories and strategies, *Reading*, **25**(1), 33–7.

Michael, J. (1986) Self-selected spelling, *Academic Therapy*, **21**(5), 557–63.

Miller, L. (1987) Spelling and handwriting, in J. Choate, T. Bennet, B. Enright, L. Miller, J. Poteet and T. Rakes, *Assessing and Programming Basic Curriculum Skills*. Boston, MA: Allyn and Bacon.

Moseley, D. (1987) Words you want to learn, *British Journal of Special Education*, **14**(2), 59–62.

Oxley, L. and Topping, K. (1990) Peer-tutored Cued Spelling with seven- to nine-year-olds, *British Educational Research Journal*, **16**(1), 63–78.

Pressley, M. (1990) *Cognitive Strategy Instruction*. Cambridge, MA: Brookline.

Read, C. (1975) *Children's Categories of Speech Sounds in English*. Urbana, IL: National Council of Teachers of English.

Scheid, K. (1993) *Helping Students Become Strategic Learners*. Cambridge, MA: Brookline.

Schlagel, R. (1989) Constancy and change in spelling development, *Reading Psychology*, **10**(3), 207–29.

Schunk, D.H. (1987) Self-efficacy and motivated learning, in N. Hastings and J. Schwieso (eds) *New Directions in Educational Psychology, Vol. 2: Behaviour and Motivation in the Classroom*. Lewes, Sussex: Falmer Press.

Scoble, J. (1988) Cued Spelling in adult literacy – a case study, *Paired Reading Bulletin*, **4**, 93–6.

   (1989) Cued Spelling and Paired Reading in adult basic education in Ryedale, *Paired Learning*, **5**, 57–62.

Scoble, J., Topping, K. and Wigglesworth, C. (1988) Training family and friends as adult literacy tutors, *Journal of Reading*, **31**(5), 410–17.

Scruggs, T.E. and Laufenberg, R. (1986) Transformational mnemonic strategies for retarded learners, *Education & Training of the Mentally Retarded*, **21**(3), 165–73.

Slavin, R.E. (1990) *Co-operative Learning: Theory, Research and Practice*, Englewood Cliffs, NJ: Prentice Hall.

Templeton, S. and Bear, D. (eds) (1992) *Development of Orthographic Knowledge and the Foundations of Literacy*. New York: Lawrence Erlbaum.

Topping, K.J. (1988) *The Peer Tutoring Handbook: Promoting Co-operative Learning*. London: Croom Helm; Cambridge, MA: Brookline.

(1995) Cued Spelling: a powerful technique for parent and peer tutoring, *The Reading Teacher* (IRA), **48**(5), 374–83.

Turner, I.F. and Quinn, E. (1986) Learning English spellings: strategies employed by primary school boys, *Educational Psychology*, **6**, 231–41.

Veit, D.T., Scruggs, T.E. and Mastropieri, M.A. (1986) Extended mnemonic instruction with learning disabled students, *Journal of Educational Psychology*, **78**(4), 300–308.

Vernon, P.E. (1977) *Graded Word Spelling Test*. Sevenoaks, Kent: Hodder and Stoughton.

Vincent, D. and Claydon, J. (1981) *Diagnostic Spelling Test*. Windsor: NFER-Nelson.

Watt, J.M. and Topping, K.J. (1993) Cued Spelling: a comparative study of parent and peer tutoring, *Educational Psychology in Practice*, **9**(2), 95–103.

Wong, B.Y.L. (1986) A cognitive approach to teaching spelling, *Exceptional Children*, **53**(2), 169–73.

Young, D. (1976) The *SPAR reading and spelling tests*. London: Hodder and Stoughton.

Note

The Paired Reading and Paired Learning Bulletins are available on loan internationally from the Educational Resources Information Centre (ERIC) through any library (microfiche reference numbers: 1985 ED285124, 1986 ED285125, 1987 ED285126, 1988 ED298429, 1989 ED313656).

Part Three
Paired Writing

CHAPTER 9

What Is Paired Writing?

'(The Writer), if the work is difficult, feels alone and sometimes even abandoned. But . . . that which is named loneliness is probably more nearly ineffectiveness, a form of failure, or form of fear . . .'

William Saroyan, 1961
(quoted in the Wisconsin Writing Project)

Paired Writing is a system for parent or peer tutoring (or co-composition) of any sort of writing (creative or technical) – in any language. The notion that writing, like reading, must have a life, application, purposes and audiences beyond classwork and, indeed, beyond school is now accepted as a 'mainstream' idea (e.g. National Curriculum Council 1990).

Poor or beginning writers are most likely to have difficulties in ideas generation, text organization and meta-cognitive knowledge of the writing process (Englert and Raphael 1988). Paired Writing specifically supports these aspects – although it is not, of course, just for 'poor writers'.

It is, naturally, similar to Paired Reading and Cued Spelling. Paired Writing is a framework and set of guidelines to be followed by pairs working together to generate a piece of writing for any purpose they wish. The aim is that the pair produce better quality writing together than they each would if working separately. (The whole should be more than the sum of its parts!) Writing is about communication, so to write more is not necessarily better – it is the quality that counts in effective communication.

The framework and the interaction between the pair are designed to result in a higher proportion of time actually spent 'on-task' – reducing to the minimum dithering, head-scratching, staring out of the window and blind panic at the sight of a blank piece of paper.

There is a great emphasis on continuity – the pair stimulating each other to keep going at any threatened hiatus. There is also a great deal of in-built constant feedback and cross-checking – what is written must make sense to both members of the pair.

The system is designed to be supportive and eliminate the fear of failure. Anxiety about peripheral aspects of writing such as spelling or punctuation should thereby be reduced to an appropriate level, and these aspects dealt with in an orderly way. As the 'best copy' is a joint effort of the pair, criticism as well as praise from external evaluators is shared.

Peer evaluation is incorporated, relieving the supervising professional of the burden of 'marking' innumerable scripts after the event (sometimes so long after that the feedback given is totally ineffective). Research shows that peer evaluation is at least as effective as teacher evaluation.

The professionals involved have a broad organizational role – they need to train the pairs, monitor subsequent practice to ensure the system is being used properly, and be on hand to help resolve any problems arising as well as give praise.

The pairs can be children working with other children in school, parents working with their own children at home, or non-professional volunteers working with children in school. Adults needing help with basic literacy also recruit pair support from spouses, parents, children, friends, neighbours and workmates, and do Paired Writing at home, at work or elsewhere. Sometimes adults attending Basic Literacy classes do Paired Writing on a peer-tutored basis in the class itself.

Paired Writing is usually operated in pairs where one member (the helper) is more skilful at writing than the other (the writer). However, the system is fairly durable and a differential in writing skill in the pair is not essential, so long as they edit carefully and use a dictionary to check spellings.

The system may be used in creative writing or English composition, or in descriptive or technical writing (e.g. writing up a science experiment or field trip), or as part of cross-curricular project work. It can also be used as part of foreign language teaching.

A Paired Writing project may be designed to mesh in with, and follow on from, direct instruction from a professional teacher on structural aspects of the writing process such as syntax, grammar, etc. However, it may equally be operated on an *ad hoc* basis as the need arises, once pairs are trained and practised in its use.

Frequency of usage of Paired Writing need not be prescribed for an initial intensive period. During the week immediately after training, it is important that pairs use the system at least three times to consolidate their practice and become fluent in the method. After this, the frequency of usage of the method may vary greatly from pair to pair according to their own situation and purposes. Teachers may still choose to prescribe an initial intensive 'commitment' period with some groups, however.

The Paired Writing System

Paired Writing consists of:

> 6 Steps
> +
> 10 Questions (Ideas)
> 5 Stages (Drafting)
> 4 Levels (Editing)

As with Cued Spelling, a flowchart outlining the system is provided for initial training and subsequent reference. Refer to this flowchart as you read this section of this chapter. The flowchart (PWR1) may be reproduced for your own purposes.

Also as with Cued Spelling, it looks more complicated than it actually proves in practice. The 'helper' is the tutor, the 'writer' is the tutee.

Step 1   Ideas Generation

The helper stimulates ideas by raising the stimulus words listed under Questions (see flowchart) with the writer, not necessarily in the order listed. These are the ten Ideas Questions.

As the writer responds verbally, the helper makes one-word rough notes. As this proceeds, the helper may recapitulate previous ideas before presenting the next stimulus word.

The helper may also think up new stimulus words not listed as ideas develop. (There are actually only nine Questions listed, plus a blank or 'wild card' option to indicate that helpers can think up their own.) The flowchart also indicates a 'What Next' loop with a further four suggested conjunction Questions which the helper may wish to use.

It is unlikely that the Ideas will be verbalized in exactly the 'right' or best-organized order straight away. Before moving on to the next Step, it is helpful for the pair to review the Ideas notes and see if the order should be changed.

This can be indicated by numbering the Ideas. Alternatively, the Ideas may seem to fall into obvious sections which can be dealt with in turn. Such sections could be colour coded and Ideas belonging to them underlined with a coloured pencil. Pairs may also choose to draw lines linking or around related Ideas, so that a 'semantic map' is constructed. Other expressions which have been used for organizing ideas in this way include Mind Maps, Word Webs, Skeleton Plans, Clustering and so on. All of these are very valuable ways of organizing Ideas before rushing on to writing continuously. All of them make the pair really think.

Step 2   Drafting

The rough Ideas notes should be placed where both members of the pair can easily see them. Drafting then proceeds. The sequence of the content is put down in continuous prose. This is done without concern for spelling, punctuation or grammatical perfection. Legibility is desirable, however, as is double-spaced writing to allow for subsequent editing. Most pairs will do better with lined paper and pencils rather than pens.

The writer considers the notes and dictates, sentence by sentence, what he or she wishes to communicate. Which of the pair actually writes this down is governed by their choice of 1 of the 5 Stages of Support (see the flowchart). The pair may choose a Stage to apply to the whole session or just to a small section of the task. For a 'harder' piece of writing, they are likely to choose a low (numbered) stage, for an 'easier' assignment a high (numbered) stage. The pair do need to make a definite decision to start off – this can always be amended later if necessary.

However, they may go back one stage (or more) when encountering a particularly 'hard' bit. In any event, if the writer can't proceed within 10 seconds, the helper must go back a stage on that problem word to give more support. There is great emphasis on keeping going, and not getting 'bogged down'. Keeping going with more support is much better than struggling for ages with less support.

Step 3   Reading

The helper then reads the Draft out loud, with as much expression and attention to punctuation as possible, while the helper and the writer look at the text together. The writer then follows this example. If the writer reads a word incorrectly, the helper immediately says that word correctly for the writer.

Some pairs like to repeat this Step after Step 4 (Editing). An alternative might be to have the writer only reading at Step 3 and the helper only repeat reading after Step 4.

Step 4   Editing

Helper and writer look at the Draft together, and the writer considers where he or she thinks improvements are necessary. The problem words, phrases or sentences may be marked with another coloured pen, pencil or highlighter.

There are four suggested criteria for assessment of the Draft – these are the 4 Edit Levels.

The most important criterion of need for improvement is where *meaning* is unclear. The second most important is to do with the organization of the separate ideas in the text, or the *order* in which meanings are presented. This could refer to organization within a phrase or sentence, or organization of the order of sentences.

PRR1 Paired Writing Flowchart

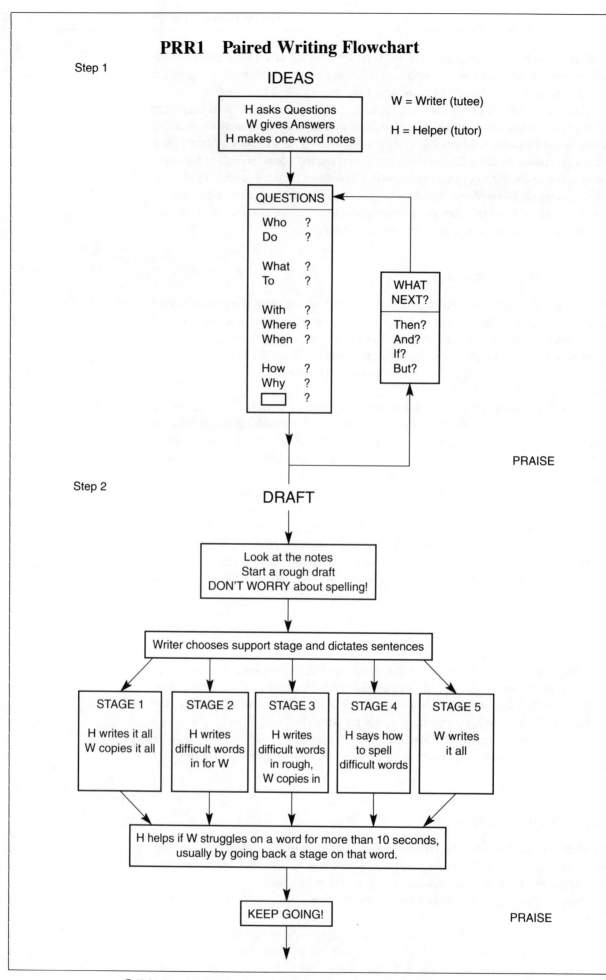

Step 1

IDEAS

H asks Questions
W gives Answers
H makes one-word notes

W = Writer (tutee)

H = Helper (tutor)

QUESTIONS

Who	?
Do	?
What	?
To	?
With	?
Where	?
When	?
How	?
Why	?
☐	?

WHAT NEXT?

Then?
And?
If?
But?

PRAISE

Step 2

DRAFT

Look at the notes
Start a rough draft
DON'T WORRY about spelling!

Writer chooses support stage and dictates sentences

| STAGE 1 | STAGE 2 | STAGE 3 | STAGE 4 | STAGE 5 |
| H writes it all W copies it all | H writes difficult words in for W | H writes difficult words in rough, W copies in | H says how to spell difficult words | W writes it all |

H helps if W struggles on a word for more than 10 seconds, usually by going back a stage on that word.

KEEP GOING!

PRAISE

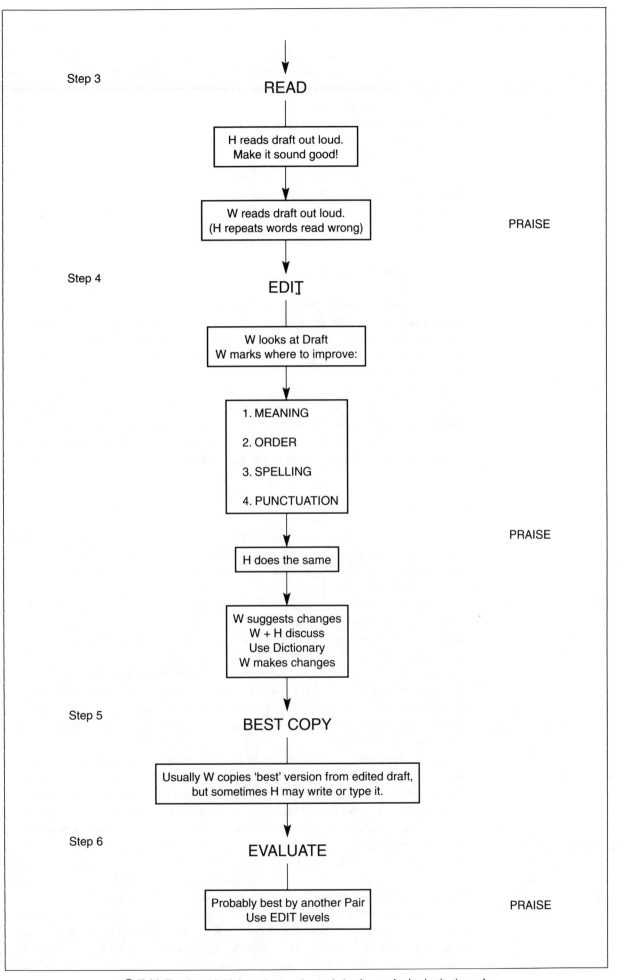

Step 3   READ

H reads draft out loud.
Make it sound good!

W reads draft out loud.
(H repeats words read wrong)   PRAISE

Step 4   EDIT

W looks at Draft
W marks where to improve:

1. MEANING

2. ORDER

3. SPELLING

4. PUNCTUATION
                                                                PRAISE
H does the same

W suggests changes
W + H discuss
Use Dictionary
W makes changes

Step 5   BEST COPY

Usually W copies 'best' version from edited draft,
but sometimes H may write or type it.

Step 6   EVALUATE

Probably best by another Pair
Use EDIT levels   PRAISE

The next consideration is whether *spellings* are correct, and the last whether *punctuation* is helpful and correct. Some writers may wish to inspect the draft four times, checking to a different criterion on each occasion, especially when they are first learning to use the system.

The helper praises the writer for completion of this (demanding) task, then marks any areas the writer has 'missed', while bearing in mind the subjective nature of some aspects of 'quality' in writing.

The writer can then make any additional suggestions about changes. The pair discuss the best correction to make, and when agreement is reached the new version is inserted in the text (preferably by the writer). Spellings over which there is the slightest doubt in the pair should be referred to the dictionary.

Step 5   Best copy

The writer then usually copies out a 'neat' or 'best' version of the corrected draft – using a pen. Sometimes the helper may write or type or word-process the piece, however, depending on the skill and stamina levels of the writer. There is no reason why members of the pair could not take turns to write sections of the best copy, to share the boredom.

The actual physical act of writing is considered the least important Step in Paired Writing, so it does not really matter who does it. The important thing is the quality of thinking and communication in the process. The best copy is a joint product of the pair. It follows that both should have their names on it. A photocopy might need to be made to enable each member of the pair to have their own copy.

Step 6   Evaluate

The pair should then inspect and consider the best copy. Given the effort they have jointly expended, they are likely to think their co-composed text is really rather good, and be happy to congratulate each other as members of a successful team of two (or 'composing duet').

However, external evaluation by assessors less likely to be wearing rose-tinted spectacles is also highly desirable. Peer evaluation is a useful mutual learning experience. Assessment by another pair is probably best, and can proceed by reference to the criteria encompassed in the Edit Levels.

Where Paired Writing occurs between children in a school setting, the first two pairs to finish can exchange best copies for mutual evaluation – this should temper any inclination to be over-critical. Positive evaluative comments must outnumber non-positive comments, and non-positive comments should be expressed in overtly subjective and sensitive terms.

This involvement in the evaluation of the work of others is of course intended to improve the self-evaluation skills of both members of each pair. These skills should then transfer to new situations, including those when the writer is writing alone.

Especially during reciprocal tutoring, the helper and writer roles may blur to some extent. The flowchart of the Paired Writing system is linear for ease of immediate understanding. However, early conceptions of the writing process as a series of sequential steps (e.g. Graves 1983) have been moderated by more organic models emphasizing recursive components which communicate with, feedback to and interrupt each other at various points (e.g. Hayes and Flower 1980).

This blurring of roles is no bad thing if it counteracts any tendency for helpers to become overly didactic. However, do not let roles slip too far or the pair will degenerate into a muddle or, worse still, an argument. Each should be and remain clear about their own 'job description'. Emphasize that 'helpers are to help writers to help themselves, *not* do everything *for* them.'

Also emphasize that there are not necessarily any 'right answers' about what constitutes 'good' writing. So helpers should avoid direct criticism of the writer's efforts, but instead make comments about their own subjective reaction, e.g. 'I find that bit hard to understand – can we think of a clearer way to write it?'

Helpers (and evaluators) must praise 'good bits' more than they draw attention to problems, e.g. 'that's an interesting word', 'I like the way you put that, it's really clear'. Praise must be given at least at the end of each Step. Praise points are indicated on the flowchart.

Additional Elements

Additions and/or adaptations can be made to the system to render it more suitable for particular circumstances. For instance, Paired Writing can be linked with Cued Spelling to ensure writers have a minimal level of skill in the accurate and swift free writing of high-frequency words.

At Step 3 Read, the full Paired Reading technique could be used if necessary or desirable by those pairs familiar with it.

At Step 4 Edit, additional editing levels could be included to extend the complexity and depth of analysis of the draft. This might be particularly desirable with more sophisticated participants, especially when generating 'creative' writing.

Thus, for instance, a Level 1a 'Wording' could be introduced to encourage pairs to deploy more interesting, varied and precise vocabulary. A Level 2a 'Grammar' could be concerned with syntactical structure. If considered important, a Level 3a 'Capitalization' could be introduced. Level 4 'Punctuation' could also be taken to include Paragraphing. Equally, a Level 5a 'Handwriting' could be introduced, to encourage pairs to improve legibility and formation of handwriting as well as general presentation.

More subtle edit levels might include 5b 'Purpose' (considering appropriateness for aims and audience specified), 5c 'Ideas Quality' (considering originality and creativity) and/or 5d 'Focus' (considering semantic density, repetition and redundancy). However, take care not to make the system too complex too soon, or pairs will increasingly depart from it or begin to skip sections.

These possible elaborations on the basic Edit Levels are listed below:

EDIT LEVELS
1. MEANING   1a Wording
2. ORDER   2a Grammar
3. SPELLING   3a Capitalization
4. PUNCTUATION   4a Paragraphing
5.   5a Handwriting
                 5b Purpose
                 5c Ideas Quality
                 5d Focus

The additional Edit Levels might also be used in Step 6 'Evaluate', or perhaps only be used in Step 6.

Other permutations and applications readily present themselves. For novelty, pairs might alternate roles during Step 1 (Ideas) even during a single session, so each member of the pair is 'thinker' and 'stimulator-recorder' in turn – particularly if the pair is writing fiction.

It may be possible to operate Paired Writing directly onto a word processor, which could prove much swifter. However, consideration would have to be given to how the pair could mark or 'flag' those parts of the text they wished to edit – perhaps by inserting extra spaces on either side of the item in doubt.

Remember that Paired Writing is 'co-composition' – both members of the pair 'own' the finished product. If copies have to be submitted individually for further external assessment or inclusion in a portfolio of achievements, each member of the pair should have a copy. Hopefully this will not play havoc with the photocopying bill – only make extra copies if absolutely essential.

Where Does Paired Writing Fit?

Clearly, there is little new about Paired Writing. It includes elements of process writing which have long been considered standard in developing better writers: Drafting, Editing, Best Copy. Beyond these, Step 1 merely offers a helping framework for the generation of ideas which is uncontroversial and capable of adaptation to individual need.

Perhaps peer assessment or evaluation (in Step 6) will be found a little more unusual by some teachers, who may be concerned about the validity, reliability and possible social repercussions of this. Of course, peer assessment which was uni-lateral and did not specify any criteria for assessment would be highly undesirable. But Paired Writing is not like that.

Pairs evaluate each other according to prescribed and familiar criteria, so motiva-tion to be positive as well as analytical is maximized. Of course, peer assessment is also expected to have a reflexive impact on the next piece of writing done by the evaluators as well as the evaluatees – an example of learning by assessment as well as learning by teaching.

The validity and reliability of the peer assessments can be expected to be as good as that of most teachers. Research has long since shown this to be so (for example Pierson 1967, Lagana 1972, Karegianes *et al.* 1980, Weeks and White 1982, MacArthur *et al.* 1991). Teachers usually want to assess a few sample pieces of Paired Writing themselves for reassurance about validity and reliability, however.

Once the system is in full swing, teachers should be freed of a huge burden of assessment of writing and offering feedback on it. With Paired Writing, assessment and feedback is built into the process of generating the text. It is thus much swifter and more immediate and therefore more effective.

Paired Writing also improves the self-evaluation skills of both members of each pair. These skills should then transfer to new situations, including those when either member of the pair is writing alone. This feature links with work on self-instructional strategy training in writing (for example, Graham and Harris 1989).

Teachers may also find the low priority given to producing the 'best copy' in Paired Writing somewhat unusual. Certainly written communication is useless unless it is legible to the intended audience. But the production of a best copy is essentially a mechanical act in Paired Writing. Tasks like these will shortly be taken over by machines – voice activated word processors (you talk to it and it prints out what you say). In Paired Writing, the *important* parts of creating new text are the thinking Steps 1, 2 and 4. They will never be taken over by machines.

The collaborative nature of Paired Writing is not at all novel. Cooperative writing groups of various sorts have been operated in primary (elementary) schools, high schools, colleges and higher education for many years. Quite often this collab-oration has occurred in larger groups than pairs, however. Also, this collaboration might have encompassed only a part of the writing process, rather than taking the whole piece through from start to finish and including evaluation.

Saunders (1989) outlined various dimensions of 'co-writing' (where peers col-laborate on every task), 'co-publishing' (in which individuals produce a collabora-tive text based on individual texts), 'co-responding' (where individuals interact only during the revising process) and 'helping' (where writers voluntarily help one another during the writing process in an *ad hoc* manner).

Writing alone is learned in the school system. Paired Writing capitalizes on the natural inclinations of children to help each other. Carr and Allen's (1987) study found that children as young as five can elicit help from each other during the writing process and that peers provided direct teaching when asked for help.

In Daiute's (1989) study of 9–12-year-olds, children wrote collaborative stories with a partner. Pairs engaged in discussion which was partly planful (organizing and controlled) and partly playful (exploring concepts and imagery). The writing of the participants improved when there was a balance between planful and playful discussion.

Collaborative writing among college and university students has also generated a substantial literature. Henschen and Sidlow (1990) have surveyed the use of collaborative writing programmes in universities in the USA. A number of such establishments have Writing Centers which deploy peer tutors (e.g. Rizzolo 1982, Rasool and Tatum 1988, Holladay 1990).

O'Donnell and her colleagues (1985) studied college students working cooperatively to create sets of explicit instructions. Not only did students who wrote cooperatively write more explicit instructions than a comparison group who wrote alone, but the subjects who worked together initially also wrote better instructions alone than those who initially wrote alone.

Nystrand (1986) compared several college classrooms. He found that students who responded in a group to one another's writing regarded the exercise as substantive reconceptualization of the text, whereas those who worked alone were concerned only with the mechanics of editing. The interactive students were engaged in more relevant cognitive conflict and task engagement than those who worked alone.

Amongst the many other publications on collaborative writing, James (1981), Christensen and her colleagues (1982), Graves (1983), Kelly *et al.* (1984), Gere (1987), Bishop (1988), Whittaker and Salend (1991) and Dale (1993) are worth reading.

Consideration of where Paired Writing 'fits' involves consideration of where writing *per se* fits into school, college and everyday life. Writing has a number of purposes and often these become confused. Writing might be used for creating, for communicating, for recording or for assessment of thought processes, to name just a few possible purposes. Paired Writing lends itself well to creating, communicating and recording. It also promotes deeper understanding by requiring participants to structure their thoughts.

Very often in our schools writing has been used too much for assessment purposes – to check whether students have thought, understood, remembered. That is why some teachers are anxious about giving away the 'marking' or grading of written assignments to peer evaluation. The use of writing as a form of outcome evaluation is actually very cumbersome and inefficient.

Paired Writing makes evaluation an integral part of the learning process, without giving it excess emphasis, without burdening the teacher and without turning children into surrogate teachers.

It is also common in schools for all children in a class to be expected to produce a piece of writing on a given subject. Paired Writing accommodates to this perfectly well, but can also easily be used in a situation where each pair chooses their own different topic.

If the whole class has to write on the same subject, the teacher will often choose to precede the Paired Writing with some whole class or group discussion, brain-storming or other stimulation. Pairs can of course be paired to create conference groups of four. Rayers (1987) has referred to activities in these larger groups as 'Shared Writing'. Some teachers like to heighten the writers' sense of purpose and audience by having some children (or pairs) read their composition to the whole class, perhaps from a specially designated 'author's chair'.

Many teachers take great trouble to establish a sense of purpose and audience for writing in many other ways, for example writing stories, letters or 'buddy journals' for children in other classes, other schools, other countries, or to parents, community personalities and agencies, or by producing information booklets, local or family histories, newsletters or newspapers. All of these are valuable components of a whole language or language experience approach to literacy. Paired Writing fits in well with all of them.

It is also worth remembering that just as Paired Reading can be done in any language and from bilingual texts, so Paired Writing might prove a powerful way of enabling children to express themselves in their language of greatest written proficiency whilst also learning to write in their second language.

In fact, just as with Paired Reading and Cued Spelling, the potential different applications for Paired Writing are very numerous.

CHAPTER 10

How To Organize and Evaluate Paired Writing

The Context and Objectives for a Paired Writing project must be considered carefully. Is Paired Writing to be targeted on many types of writing for many purposes, or just one? Starting with a restricted focus would be prudent, especially if the work can be organized and monitored by one enthusiastic teacher. Given success in a restricted initiative, the method can gradually be spread to other types of writing, other areas of the curriculum, other places, other purposes and audiences and other professional supervisors as appropriate.

Recruitment, Selection and Matching

Within schools Paired Writing is often used on a peer-tutored basis. This can be with pairs of the same age (often within the same class, which makes organization much easier) or of different ages. Where there is a differential in writing ability in the pair, it should not be too great, or the helper may become bored and/or dominant and the writer insecure and/or dependent, especially if they are fixed in these roles and Paired Writing goes on for a long time. Otherwise, many of the considerations of Recruitment, Selection and Matching from Parts One and Two apply.

Do not put best friends or worst enemies in the same pair, and be careful when matching personality types who are very similar or very dissimilar. This is perhaps more important with Paired Writing than with the other paired methods.

If pairs are matched without a differential in writing skill, you might well choose to operate reciprocal tutoring. In this case, the roles of writer and helper are best alternated after the completion of each piece of writing.

Materials

Each pair must have a system flowchart, two pens or pencils, rough paper for drafting, easy access to a dictionary of the appropriate level and good-quality paper for a best copy. It is strongly recommended that the use of erasers is heavily discouraged. Coloured pens, pencils or highlighters for editing may be found helpful. Supervising professionals should decide whether lined or unlined paper is appropriate for each pair.

Entry Skills

Writers (tutees) should minimally: (a) know what a sentence is, (b) be able to read the flowchart and their draft, (c) be able to copywrite legibly, and also preferably (d) be able to write letter sounds and/or names to dictation (although this could be taught as a parallel exercise).

Helpers (tutors) should minimally have: (a) adequate receptive and expressive language, (b) the ability to write relatively simple single words legibly, (c) the ability to read simple continuous prose, preferably with a degree of expression, (d) some minimal competence in spelling and punctuation, and (e) the ability to use a simple dictionary (although this could be taught as a parallel exercise).

Training

Pairs must be properly trained in the use of the system. Hold a training session at which participants sit in their pairs with the required materials at hand. Describe the system, referring to the flowchart. Each pair must have a hard copy of the flowchart during the training session, which they will keep for subsequent reference. You may also wish to show the chart on an overhead projector in enlarged sections.

Demonstrating Paired Writing involves the audience in seeing a lot of intricate written detail as well as listening carefully to the discussions of the model pair. If you use video modelling, the video will have to be very carefully made. Role play between professionals or between a teacher and a child may well be the easiest way.

Choose a very brief and self-contained writing task for the demonstration, like writing some instructions. The pair can operate standing by an overhead projector and use this to show their notes at each stage. Prepared lined acetate sheets are a good idea. The demonstrating pair need to ensure that deliberate 'mistakes' are made at Ideas and Draft Stages, to show how writers are supported through these.

To allow every practising pair to think up their own topic for practice would be unmanageable. Specify a very brief and self-contained writing task for this purpose for all of them. Writing some simple instructions always works well and some humour often results. Examples include 'How To Strike A Match', 'How To Tie Your Shoelaces' and 'How To Fill A Hot Water Bottle'. Keep it very simple – everything turns out much more complicated and time-consuming than you would imagine.

Have the pairs practise the system while you circulate to monitor technique. Emphasize that helpers should not be too directive. Allow at least an hour for the training session.

Where complex Edit Levels are used, further training of pairs will be necessary. A sample of writing can be displayed on the overhead projector and edited as a whole group exercise. Pairs can then practise editing samples of their own past writing, before embarking on full Paired Writing.

Contact Organization

After training, the system will need to be used as frequently as possible for the next week or two, to ensure consolidation and promote fluency in its use and enable any problems to be picked up.

Normally teachers schedule peer-tutored Paired Writing for specific sessions within the regular timetabled English curriculum to start with. Once established, Paired Writing can be extended into other curriculum time slots for other purposes, e.g. into science and technology for recording and reporting purposes. As Paired Writing is increasingly implemented 'across the curriculum', less and less English time need be allocated for this purpose.

With peer-tutored Paired Writing in class, practical problems can include very various time requirements or noise levels in different pairs. However, you would hope for some spontaneous generalization of the procedure to preparation, home-work, break or recess or even leisure time. Should this occur, the problem of various time requirements will diminish.

You might wish to promote this generalization by offering facilities for a 'Writer's Club' or some such to meet at lunch times. Certainly it will be a good idea to let the participants know that you hope that this generalization will occur and are prepared to encourage it in any practical way you can.

Also emphasize that co-composition through Paired Writing is not 'cheating'. But take care that the participants do not generalize the method to the written home-work requirements of other teachers who *might* regard it as cheating, without discussing with those teachers first!

When Paired Writing is used in open community settings (e.g. with parents and children or adult-to-adult), an informal 'contract' regarding minimum frequency of usage should be established – e.g. Paired Writing for 3 sessions of 20 minutes per week for 3 weeks. This initial prescription is necessary to establish fluency and positive habits, particularly in previously reluctant writers.

Support, Monitoring and Feedback

Self-monitoring is a major feature of Paired Writing. Pairs are still likely to need some external monitoring and support, however, especially in the early stages.

Direct observation during peer-tutored Paired Writing sessions or during 'booster' meetings for community-based projects are desirable to check conformity to technique and advise on any necessary modifications for individual pairs. Take care not to be drawn into commenting on apparent quality of output when monitoring conformity to technique – the former is in the first instance the task and responsibility of the pair. The monitor is supervising process, not product.

Some sort of 'trouble-shooting' facility needs to be available, in case of problems, to which pairs can self-refer. Thus the 'Writer's Club' might incorporate a writing clinic or surgery, at which pairs can seek the help of a wider cross-section of their peer group with a particular problem. Such a surgery could also feature the presence of a professional at limited or alternating times.

Community-based projects would benefit from the use of some sort of diary similar to those used in Paired Reading and Cued Spelling. At the peer assessment stage you could incorporate written mutual feedback from peers. This would yield permanent written records as well as yet another purpose for writing. To scaffold this, a simple structured form using the Edit Levels as headings could be used until the procedure had become internalized by the participants.

As with the other paired methods, feedback meetings with participants to seek their views on the value of the method, any possible improvements and alternative applications will be most valuable.

Evaluation

There is clearly a need for evaluation of the effectiveness of Paired Writing, to check if it meets its objectives – the production of better-quality writing than would occur if writers worked separately.

The word 'quality' is important here. Paired Writing is not concerned with yielding a greater volume of writing, since this of itself is worthless, like reading fast without understanding.

However, measurement of 'quality' of writing is problematic. This can be approached by assessing written output against some widely accepted criteria generally considered indicative of 'good' writing. This is what teachers informally do all the time when marking or grading a piece of writing.

Even when a clearly articulated set of criteria are established, questions remain. Are the criteria actually widely accepted? Are they based on empirical research? Are they unambiguous and capable of yielding high inter-rater reliabilities? How 'objective' can the assessment of the content of creative writing ever be?

Tentative possible elements in an assessment and evaluation strategy of the 'quality indicator' type are considered in more detail below. This common frame-work could be applied to many different types of writing in many different settings.

However, there is an alternative approach to the assessment and evaluation of writing, which we may call the 'objectives' approach. Any piece of writing can be assumed to have a purpose. The purposes or objectives of a piece of writing are certainly set by its composer. However, additional and/or different objectives may also be set by the recipient of the writing, and possibly by a third party with some vested interest in the outcome (e.g. a teacher).

Disagreements about the worth of a piece of writing often stem from the different views of different involved parties about the objectives of the exercise. Frequently these differing views are not clearly (and sometimes not even honestly) articulated, so the writer is never clear what they have to do to be right. Quite often not even the audience, client or customer for the piece are specified. If the objectives of a piece of writing are discussed, negotiated and agreed at the outset, a much 'better' written result can be expected.

Clearly, if the objectives of the piece of writing are specified in this way, the writing can subsequently be evaluated with reference to these objectives. This does not, of course, remove all the subjectivity in the assessment process, but it does reduce it.

However, the 'objectives' approach to assessing writing presents difficulties from a research point of view. The objectives set for a piece of writing will reflect the idiosyncratic needs and objectives specified by the interested parties in that situation at that time. Objectives will probably be quite different in different situations. Evaluation by objectives yields multiple individual outcomes which are highly various and very difficult to summarize or aggregate. Consequently the overall general picture is hard to see, and comparisons difficult to make.

A problem with the traditional assessment of writing was that some teachers mixed the 'quality indicator' method with the 'objectives' method without realizing it. As a result, neither teacher nor child were clear enough about how the assessment was carried out, and some of the beneficial learning effects of precise feedback from the assessment process were lost.

In the rest of this chapter, the focus will switch to, and remain on, the quality indicator method. Those wishing to supplement quality indicator assessment with individualized objectives assessment will be able to use their own initiative to do so.

Quality indicator assessment

Frameworks for quality indicator assessment have been proposed by several workers in the field. Some of these will be reviewed below. Common elements will then be aggregated.

The elements you might actually use in your own project will vary in response to different situations. A relevant selection can be made from this 'item bank' of generally accepted indicators.

An early and widely known quality indicator was the 'Analytic Scale' of Diederich (1974). This is composed of eight separate categories, each scored on a five-point scale by the assessor. Categories referring to matters of content were given double-weighted scores to reflect their importance in relation to matters of form. The categories were: Ideas, Organization, Wording, Usage, Punctuation, Spelling, Handwriting – and 'Flavour'.

Cooper (1977) later promulgated a similar scale for holistic evaluation of writing, but its reliability was low. Karegianes *et al.* (1980) used a modified version of the Analytic Scale (omitting 'Flavour') and found adequate inter-rater reliability (coefficients of 0.87 at pretest and 0.85 at post-test) between two experienced English teachers when assessing essays all of which were on the same topic.

Carlson and Roellich (1983) developed an 11-item scale named the 'Indicator for Rating Performance, Grades 6–12'. This was intended to be used by children during peer assessment. Differing numbers of points could be awarded by raters in each category, thus: Purpose (10 points), Information (20), Organization (15), Variety and Precision of Language (10), Grammatical Completeness, Clarity and Variety (15), Usage (5), Capitalization (5), Punctuation (5), Spelling (10), Legibility and Presentation (5), Originality and Creativity (10). Complex definitions and simple Evaluation Score Sheets were provided. There is no evidence of reliability nor information about the basis of the differential points system.

Isaacson (1988) considered the five most important assessment dimensions for writing to be Fluency, Content, Conventions, Syntax and Vocabulary. He notes that those assessment categories which are concerned with the superficial characteristics of a piece of writing are usually those with highest reliability, and the inclusion of many such categories in a total scale artificially inflates its apparent reliability.

Fluency is defined as the number of words written (presumably in any given time), Content as originality of ideas, organization of thought, coherence, awareness of audience and maturity of style, Conventions as spelling, margins, punctuation, handwriting, capitalization, micro-grammar (e.g. word endings), Syntax as macro-grammar (length and complexity of sentences), and Vocabulary as originality and maturity in choice of words (relative to own previous performance).

Although Isaacson (1988) refers to much background research, no evidence is given from field trials of his own conclusions. This is also true of the error analysis system described by Goodman *et al.* (1987), which was preoccupied with deficits rather than competencies.

Contributions from a behavioural perspective have come from Hopman and Glynn (1988, 1989). These workers review research demonstrating that many aspects of writing behaviour can be improved simply by specifying the required behaviour and positively reinforcing it. Aspects which have been improved in this way include handwriting speed and legibility, capitalization, punctuation, use of prepositional phrases and other parts of speech. Correspondence training (self-verbalization before action) has also produced good results (e.g. Hopman and Glynn 1989).

Nor have these positive effects been confined to aspects of form and mechanics in writing which have preoccupied teachers for centuries. A number of studies (e.g. Glover and Gary 1976, Harrop and McCann 1984) have shown improvements in fluency (number of different written productions), flexibility (number of verb forms), number of words per production and originality, supported by gains on tests of creative thinking.

Graham and Harris (1989) have made a number of contributions to this field. These authors note that learning-disabled children often have a production problem rather than the wider information processing problem which may be all too readily assumed. Thus, MacArthur and Graham (1987) found that learning-disabled children's dictated compositions were three to four times longer than their hand-written or word-processed papers.

The written compositions of learning-disabled children are characterized by the omission of critical structural content elements (e.g. how the story ends) and the inclusion of much irrelevant or nonfunctional information. Pre-writing planning, a sense of audience and overall cohesiveness is often lacking. Accordingly, Graham and Harris (1989) sought to train such children in self-instructional strategic prompting procedures (somewhat similar to correspondence training).

Changes in writing performance were analysed through measures of functional elements (premise, reasons, conclusions, elaborations), nonfunctional elements, number of words written and cohesiveness. Scoring procedures for these were largely based on those developed previously by Scardamalia *et al.* (1982). Reliability coefficients were: total number of elements 0.89, premise 0.77, reasons 0.79, conclusions 1.00, elaborations 0.83, nonfunctional 0.97, coherence 0.83 and number of words 0.99. These are certainly adequately high, but replication at these levels from other sites would be welcome.

Additionally, pre-writing time was recorded. A scale developed by Graham and Harris (1989) for assessing the schematic structure of stories was also applied. This scored eight story elements: Main character, Locale, Time, Starter event, Goal, Action, Ending and Reaction. (Of course, this scale would be of limited utility with non-fiction writing.) Generalization to a new setting and maintenance of improvements over time were also assessed. The self-image as a writer of the participants was investigated on a before and after basis.

Considering all the analytical categories which have been proposed in the literature, one might expect to find greater agreement on the more readily measurable aspects of form and convention than on those of creativity, originality and communicative content. This is indeed the case, although there is also a good deal of agreement on issues of content.

Common elements in the item bank of quality indicators can be divided into those referring to content and those referring to form.

Content

1.   Purpose and Awareness of Audience
2.   Originality and Creativity of Ideas
3.   Organization and Coherence of Structure
4.   Variety and Precision of Wording

Form

5.   Legibility of Handwriting
6.   Speed and Volume of Production
7.   Grammar
8.   Spelling
9.   Punctuation
10. Capitalization

If the temptation to use this apparently tidy 10 point scale is overwhelming, remember the relative importance of content and form. You may wish to double score the content items to counterbalance this (cf. Diederich 1974).

Also remember that some of these aspects are not considered particularly relevant in Paired Writing (e.g. 5 and 6), or are taken as read (no pun intended). Paired Writing should not be expected necessarily to result in improvements in these aspects.

Be under no illusions that this scale is magically scientific. It is based on more evidence than is what most teachers traditionally do. Nevertheless, it is capable of generating worthless results if used in too casual a manner. Ideally, carry out your own local reliability check on a small sample of scripts, which are rated by yourself and a colleague without knowledge of their originators. Only when you have reached at least 70 per cent agreement can you begin to feel your results are reasonably reliable.

Even with a relatively reliable scale, the major problem with the assessment of writing is the enormous consumption of time involved. The only redeeming feature is that probably you would have had to mark or grade those scripts anyhow, albeit in less detail. Because of the time-consuming nature of this kind of evaluation, little has been published on the effectiveness of Paired Writing using such methods. This gap in the literature will hopefully soon be filled – maybe by you!

Standardized testing

Teachers might have doubts about whether a norm-referenced test can provide valid and reliable measures of writing ability. However, such instruments do exist. At least they incorporate relatively consistent dimensions for assessment.

Lagana (1972) used the STEP Writing Test and STEP Essay Test as pre-test and post-test measures with experimental and control groups in a writing experiment involving both individualized learning and peer-group learning. On both tests the experimental group performed significantly better at post-test than the control group who had received 'traditional' composition instruction. Experimental subjects made particular gains in 'Organization, Critical Thinking and Appropriateness'. The test results were supplemented with more 'subjective' data.

The Woodcock-Johnson Psychoeducational Battery (Woodcock 1977) includes a Written Language Achievement Cluster, relating performance in writing to the subject's intellectual ability in other respects. This is obviously an extremely crude diagnostic indicator.

The Test of Written Language (Hammill and Larsen 1983) is another example of this genre. This covers five elements of written expression: Mechanics of handwriting, Meaningful content, Convention conformity (spelling, capitalization, punctuation), Syntactical structure and Creative (or cognitive) component. An over-emphasis on mechanics and form is evident, despite evidence of very low correlations between grammatical knowledge and quality of written output (Kuykendall 1975).

Separate standardized tests of restricted aspects of the writing process such as spelling, punctuation, capitalization and understanding of vocabulary can also be found. In the UK, the Bristol Achievement Tests (Brimer 1969) go a little further and include subtests of paragraph meaning, sentence organization and organization of ideas.

How these subskill tests relate to the total organic writing process is another question. It should be noted that these instruments are not founded on satisfactory or recent theory and research about the writing process.

Structured subjective feedback

As with the other paired methods, verbal feedback can be solicited from participants in a variety of settings, but is often difficult to summarize. A simple reproducible Paired Writing feedback questionnaire which can be used by both tutors and tutees will be found in Part Four Section C (PWR2).

References

Bishop, W. (1988) Helping peer writing groups succeed, *Teaching English in the Two-Year College*, **15**(2), 120–5.

Brimer, A. (1969) *Bristol Achievement Tests*. Windsor: NFER-Nelson.

Carlson, D.M. and Roellich, C. (1983) Teaching writing easily and effectively to get results. Part 11: The evaluation process. Paper presented at Annual Meeting of the National Council of Teachers of English, Seattle, 14–16 April 1983 (ERIC ED233372).

Carr, E. and Allen, J. (1987) Peer teaching and learning during writing time in kindergarten. Paper presented at the National Reading Conference, St Petersburg, Fla., December 1987.

Christensen, L., Haugen, N.S. and Kean, J.M. (eds) (1982) *A Guide to Teaching Self/Peer Editing*. Madison, WI: School of Education, University of Wisconsin (ERIC ED249513).

Cooper, C.R. (1977) Holistic evaluation of writing, in C.R. Cooper and L. Odell (eds) *Evaluating Writing: Describing, Measuring, Judging*, Buffalo, NY: State University of New York and National Council of Teachers of English.

Daiute, C. (1989) Play as thought: thinking strategies of young writers, *Harvard Educational Review*, **59**(1), 1–23.

Dale, H. (1993) Conflict and engagement: collaborative writing in one ninth-grade classroom. Paper presented at the Annual Conference of the American Educational Research Association, Atlanta, GA, April 1993.

Diederich, P. (1974) *Measuring Growth in English*. Urbana, IL: National Council of Teachers of English.

Englert, C. and Raphael, T. (1988) Constructing well-formed prose: process, structure and metacognitive knowledge, *Exceptional Children*, **54**, 513–20.

Gere, A.R. (1987) *Writing Groups: History, Theory, Implications*. Carbondale IL: Southern Illinois University Press.

Glover, J. and Gary, A.L. (1976) Procedures to increase some aspects of creativity, *Journal of Applied Behavior Analysis*, **9**, 79–84.

Goodman, L., Casciato, D. and Price, M. (1987) LD students' writing: analyzing errors, *Academic Therapy*, **22**(5), 453–61.

Graham, S. and Harris, K.R. (1989) Improving learning disabled students' skills at composing essays: self-instructional strategy training, *Exceptional Children*, **56**(3), 201–14.

Graves, D. (1983) *Writing: Teachers and Children At Work*. New York: Heinemann.

Hammill, D. and Larsen, D. (1983) *Test of Written Language*. Austin, TX: Pro Ed.

Harrop, A. and McCann, C. (1984) Modifying 'creative writing' in the classroom, *British Journal of Educational Psychology*, **54**, 62–72.

Hayes, J. and Flower, L. (1980) Identifying the organization of the writing process, in L.W. Gregg and E.R. Steinberg (eds) *Cognitive Processes in Writing*, Hillsdale, NJ: Erlbaum.

Henschen, B.M. and Sidlow, E.I. (1990) Collaborative writing, *College Teaching*, **38**(1), 29–32.

Holladay, J.M. (1990) *Writing Across the Curriculum Annual Report 1989–90*. Michigan: Monroe County Community College (ERIC ED326260).

Hopman, M. and Glynn, T. (1988) Behavioural approaches to improving written expression, *Educational Psychology*, **8**(1/2), 81–100.

(1989) The effect of correspondence training on the rate and quality of written expression of four low achieving boys, *Educational Psychology*, **9**(3), 197–213.

Isaacson, S. (1988) Assessing the writing product: qualitative and quantitative measures, *Exceptional Children*, **54**(6), 528–34.

James, D.R. (1981) Peer teaching in the writing classroom, *English Journal*, **70**(7), 48–50.

Karegianes, M.L., Pascarella, E.T. and Pflaum, S.W. (1980) The effects of peer editing on the writing proficiency of low-achieving tenth grade students, *Journal of Educational Research*, **73**(4), 203–207.

Kelly, P. et al. (1984) Composition through the team approach, *English Journal*, **73**(5), 71–4.

Kuykendall, C. (1975) Grammar and composition: myths and realities, *English Journal*, **64**, 6–7.

Lagana, J.R. (1972) The development, implementation and evaluation of a model for teaching composition which utilizes individualized learning and peer grouping. PhD thesis, University of Pittsburgh.

MacArthur, C. and Graham, S. (1987) Learning disabled students' composing under three methods of text production: handwriting, word processing and dictation, *Journal of Special Education*, **21**, 22–42.

MacArthur, C.A., Schwartz, S.S. and Graham, S. (1991) Effects of a reciprocal peer revision strategy in special education classrooms, *Learning Disabilities Research and Practice*, **6**(4), 201–210.

National Curriculum Council (1990) *Writing Partnerships 1: Home, School and Community*, Walton-on-Thames, Surrey: Thomas Nelson.

Nystrand, M. (1986) Learning to write by talking about writing: a summary of research on intensive peer review in expository writing at the University of Wisconsin-Madison, in M. Nystrand (ed.) *The Structure of Written Communication*. Orlando. FL: Academic Press.

O'Donnell, A.M., Danserau, D.F., Rocklin, T., Lambiotte, J.G. *et al.* (1985) Co-operative writing: direct effects and transfer, *Written Communication*, **2**(3), 307–15.

Pierson, H. (1967) Peer and teacher correction: a comparison of the effects of two methods of teaching composition in grade nine English classes. PhD thesis, New York University.

Rasool, J. and Tatum, T. (1988) Influencing student reality and academic performance. Unpublished paper, Freshman Year Experience Conference, East Columbia, SC.

Rayers, C. (1987) Writing should be sharing, *Reading* (UKRA), **21**(2), 115–24.

Rizzolo, P. (1982) Peer tutors make good teachers: a successful writing program, *Improving College and University Teaching*, **30**(3), 115–19.

Saunders, W.M. (1989) Collaborative writing tasks and peer interaction, *International Journal of Educational Research*, **13**(1), 101–12.

Scardamalia, M., Bereiter, C. and Goelman, H. (1982) The role of production factors in writing ability, in M. Nystrand (ed.) *What Writers Know: The Language, Process and Structure of Written Discourse*. New York: Academic Press.

Topping, K.J. (1993) Paired writing or co-composition, *Co-operative Learning*, **13**(4), 32–4.

Weeks, J.O. and White, M.B. (1982) Peer editing versus teacher editing: does it make a difference? Paper presented at Conference of North Carolina Council of the International Reading Association, Charlotte, N.C., 7–9 March 1982 (ERIC ED224014).

Whittaker, C.R. and Salend, S.J. (1991) Collaborative peer writing groups, *Reading, Writing and Learning Disabilities*, **7**, 125–36.

Woodcock, R. (1977) *The Woodcock-Johnson Psychoeducational Battery*. Allen, TX: DLM Teaching Resources.

CHAPTER 11

Designing New Paired Methods

The methods reviewed in Parts One, Two and Three are obviously not the only methods. Especially as new techniques are invented and evaluated, they might not even remain among the best methods. Creative developments which work better are to be welcomed.

So from the mass of experience and research evidence on paired methods accumulated so far, what guidelines for future developments can be extracted?

In this chapter you will find an outline of design considerations and a check list of 'engineering' criteria likely to maximize success in developing new methods for parent and peer tutoring in literacy activities. The emphasis will remain on flexible, adaptable, low technology and inexpensive procedures which are easily transmitted. Those educators inventing their own local procedures may find this helpful.

Which aspects of the learning situation can we change to yield better learning? The METTLE acronym is a handy reminder of the six main aspects: Materials, Equipment, Task, Teaching behaviour, Learning behaviour and Environment.

These six aspects can be useful when analysing classroom teaching, but here their relevance to the design of new Paired Learning methods is the focus. In the past teachers have often given undue emphasis to the importance of materials and equipment. Thus if a child was slow to learn, a 'special' reading scheme or the introduction of expensive hardware such as computers was often the first recourse. In many less wealthy countries these options are not available, but their reading standards do not necessarily suffer as much as might be expected.

It is clear that tutoring systems which are dependent on specific educational materials or equipment are unlikely to truly empower – they will be too expensive, too restricted in scope and interest and always too like a welfare hand-out, risking creating dependency. The real challenge is to design tutoring systems which can be used by anyone, anywhere, with any material which is to hand and is of interest.

The whole point of Paired Learning activities is to empower the participants for their own purposes within their own natural environment – with all its constraints. The activities need to be feasible within the natural ecology of the family or the peer group and be capable of becoming embedded and self-sustaining there. They need to be engineered to enable the pair to meet their own goals.

Paired Learning activities should thus be more concerned with the nature of the Tasks involved. For maximum motivation and sense of personal ownership, some free choice from a range of options is always to be preferred. While methods for the pair to assess the difficulty of any task can be outlined, they should decide what they feel ready to attempt.

Most crucially of all, pairs need close guidance about what the tutor should do and what the tutee should do. The options and prescriptions should be carefully thought and worked through to ensure that tutor and tutee behaviour will interact successfully at every stage. This requires careful planning. Guidelines for organization and structuring successful interaction are outlined below.

Engineering Guidelines

Objectives

What benefits is the programme expected to have? This is important for marketing, recruitment and subsequent evaluation purposes. The programme must not interfere with the regular school curriculum, but should dovetail into it. It should also capitalize on the qualitative differences and advantages of Paired Learning tutoring as compared to school instruction. Keep the objectives modest for your first attempt. Do it small and well. Engineer in success for yourself!

Ability differential

Be clear with potential Paired Learning tutors and tutees (and yourself) about the minimum and maximum competence they will need in the curriculum area of tutoring. You need to have a pretty good idea about the feasible range of ability differential which will allow the pair to function effectively given the materials and interactive behaviours involved. If tutor competence is in doubt there must be reference to some acceptable master source to verify correctness, since overlearning of errors would leave the tutee worse off than at the start.

Flexibility

The methods you choose should be able to be used without major modification by participants of different ages and abilities with different life situations and needs. Flexibility also needs to accommodate different learning styles and different ambitions in different physical environments. Clearly, the more you specify expensive and special materials, the less likely it is that these flexibility requirements will be met.

Likewise, your chosen methods should in the medium term enable and empower the pair to deploy a range of strategies, rather than strait-jacketing them into a single professionally preferred one. Activity should preferably be varied and multi-sensory, with switches between different styles of reading, listening, writing, speaking, and so on. Sustaining some novelty is important – we don't want to make it seem like boring homework!

Interaction

Methods should involve responsive interactivity from both members of the pair. Otherwise one may soon decline into being merely a checker or a passive audience and motivation will soon evaporate. The method should promote a high rate of time on task, with an emphasis on keeping going. Maintaining the flow of activity increases the number of learning opportunities and helps stave off anxiety and boredom.

Satisfaction

Likewise, both members of the pair must gain some intrinsic satisfaction from the activity. Pure altruism may be enough to get a pair started, but it will not sustain the interaction in the long run. Basically, it's got to be fun for both or all involved.

Self-management

The method should avoid any authoritarian overtones. Try to build in democracy. The tutee should have a substantial degree of control over the process of tutoring and preferably over the curriculum content and materials as well. Tutee control of the amount of support offered by the tutor is especially valuable, since otherwise tutees may feel either unsupported or constantly interrupted. Tutees and tutors should be able to exercise choice and initiative – deprived of the opportunity, they will never develop the skills.

Instructions

Should be simple, clear and above all specific. Instructions are probably best given as a series of sequential task-analysed steps in the first instance. Tutors like to be told what they have to do to be right, at least at the start. Once they have developed more confidence and understanding they will choose for themselves when to start extemporizing.

Most people dislike wordy educational philosophizing and vague and fuzzy open-ended statements. (Of course you will encounter some verbal middle-class families who prefer to talk about it than actually *do* it!) Both tutor and tutee should be given very clear (interactive) job descriptions, since without this the process of tutoring can rapidly degenerate into a muddle. The provision of a simple visual map, chart or other cues to remind the pair of how it is all supposed to work may well be helpful.

Materials

Especially for those with learning disability or delay, the curriculum materials in use should be individualized to match their needs and interests. However, try to avoid ending up depriving them of any choice. Are the materials to be completely free choice, controlled choice from ranges of difficulty or precisely specified by the professionals, or some continuum of these possibilities as the tutoring develops?

Are the materials required actually available and easy for regular access by pairs? Does the tutoring method adapt to progression on to increasingly difficult materials? Have you specified what the pair will need to have available by way of basic equipment (e.g. pen, paper, dictionary?) and ensured it will be available?

Error control

The tutee should not feel as if they are making many errors, since this is bad for morale. If this is not controlled via graded materials, careful accommodation by the tutor to the tutee's natural speed and style is necessary. The provision of swift but non-intrusive support from the helper must be a feature of the tutoring technique, without creating tutee dependency. Errors are potentially the major stress point in the tutoring relationship – but be alert to other possible causes of stress and fatigue in the system.

Error signalling

When an error is made, there should be swift feedback from the helper that this is the case. However, this feedback should not be so immediate that the tutee has no opportunity to detect the error for his or her self. Error signalling should be positive and minimally interruptive.

Error correction

A swift, simple, specific and preferably consistently applicable error correction procedure must be clearly laid down. Tutees should be encouraged in training to see this as supportive. The procedure should draw minimum attention to the error. It should distract as little as possible from the main objective of the task in hand. There should also be a strong emphasis on self-checking and self-correction, both higher order skills which need to be fostered.

Eliminate negatives

'Don't say don't' – strongly recommend positive error signalling, correction and other procedures which are *incompatible* with the negative and intrusive behaviours which might otherwise occur. It is ineffective to give a list of prohibited behaviours.

Accentuate positives

Be specific about the need for praise. Make recommendations about *what* to praise (especially self-correction and initiative-taking), *how often* to praise, *how* to praise (verbal and non-verbal aspects), and the need for variety and relevance to the task.

Deploy individual token or tangible rewards only if all else fails, since otherwise motivation and participation might well stop when the goodies run out. Some group acknowledgement of participation via badges, certificates, etc. might be valuable and acceptable, and is useful advertising. You need to manage the group ethos of your project to develop mutual support between participants – otherwise when you stop, they stop.

Discussion

Emphasize that talk is essential in the learning process. It is not 'resting' or a waste of time, if it relates to the activities at hand. It serves to promote and confirm full understanding by the participants and is 'genuine work'. It also helps avoid mechanical conformity to the surface requirements of the task by either member of the pair.

Modelling

Ensure the method includes some demonstration of competence by the tutor, which may be imitated (or even improved upon) by the tutee. Too much reliance on verbal instruction will be ineffective. Tutors should also be encouraged to model more general desirable behaviours, such as enthusiasm for the activity.

Participant pairs will also serve as models for other pairs, and the project group should deliberately be kept in contact so that the social dynamic adds a further dimension to motivation. Remember the coordinating professional must model continuing enthusiasm for the programme!

Training

Training is essential, and should be done live with both members of the pair present. Don't just rely on handing out a leaflet or a video for home study – it doesn't work. Your training session should include verbal, visual and written information-giving (bilingual if necessary). It should also have a demonstration, immediate practice with a real live activity, feedback for participants about how they did and further individual coaching for those who are struggling.

Training pairs individually is very costly of professional time. Well-organized group training can be just as effective, while also serving to develop group support and solidarity. You may need specially pre-selected materials or equipment to hand for the training meeting.

Contracting

Specify an initial trial period and be very clear about the time costs for the pair should they decide to participate. Remember activity little and often will be most effective, especially with those with learning difficulties.

Give pairs a free choice about participation – there is no point trying to persuade or bully them. However, expect pairs to clearly contract in to participation. You need to know if they are in or out of the programme – there is no halfway house. Thus participation is, of course, voluntary but needs to be seen as total and not optionally partial – otherwise the effect of your programme will quickly become diluted.

Ensure there is mutual discussion between professionals and participants about effectiveness and proposed improvements by the end of the trial period. Even if all the participants say different things, it is important that they feel consulted. Discuss continuation options and seek contract renewal by participants, possibly in a range of alternative formats. At this point pairs should be increasingly confident and capable of devising their own adaptations and creating their own novelty, and should be increasingly ambitious.

Monitoring

Emphasize self-checking. Some simple form of self-recording is desirable, and both members of the pair should participate in this. Periodic checking of these records by the co-ordinating professional takes relatively little professional time but is very valuable in making everyone feel as if they are working together.

This may need to be supplemented in at least some cases by further individual enquiry of one or both members of the pair. If the time is available, direct observation of the pair in action, either in school or at their home, can be extremely revealing and diagnostically helpful. This can be done on an individual basis with a pair who are finding particular difficulty, or in a group setting at a more general 'booster' meeting.

Evaluating

Turning from monitoring the process of Paired Learning activities to evaluating their products or outcomes, be clear as to the objectives of evaluation. There is little point in doing it for its own sake – what are you going to *do* with the results?

Feeding general data on their success back to the participants might well increase their longer-term motivation. Publicizing the data might expand subsequent recruitment or attract additional funding. But how should you review to what extent the curriculum content of the activity has actually been mastered and retained in the longer term?

Criterion-referenced tests closely allied to the tutoring process are likely to give the most valid (and most impressive) results. However, a norm-referenced test in the same general area is a more stringent test of generalization of skills acquired and might be construed as more 'objective' by outsiders. Obviously you could only use such measures with the full agreement of the participants, which may not always be forthcoming.

You might at least solicit subjective feedback from the participants on a consumer satisfaction basis. Any questionnaire or brief interview schedule will need to be designed carefully to ask very specific questions and avoid in-built positive bias. You will in any case benefit from the 'grateful testimonials' effect, but try to defend yourself from any possible criticism of being 'unscientific'. Since you don't need a lot of extra work, also remember to make it easy to score and summarize!

Comparison or control groups of non-participants are great if you can get them. Do try and save a little spare energy to collect longer-term follow-up data on at least a sub-sample, to check if there is any wash-out of gains made in the short term. However, also ensure the evaluation procedure does not overwhelm or stress the participants – or indeed yourself.

Generalization and maintenance

You will need to build in some means for continuing review, feedback and injection of further novelty and enthusiasm. Otherwise pairs will not automatically keep going and maintain the use of their skills. Again, the social dynamic of the group is important. You are likely also to need to consciously foster the broadening use of these skills to different materials and contexts for new purposes. All of this will consolidate the progress made, build confidence and empower the pair still further.

When pairs have developed sufficient awareness of effective tutoring to begin to design their own systems, you know you have done a good job. As tutees themselves recruit a wider range of tutors, the tutee becomes even more central as quality controller of the tutoring process.

Reaching the Hard-to-Reach

In peer-tutoring programmes, the raw material is always to hand (except for children who truant – but even they often turn up for their peer-tutoring session). Parent tutoring or Family Literacy programmes can have much larger recruitment problems, especially in disadvantaged areas.

Of course, some of those in need will remain unreachable, at least for now. Families who have not enjoyed a good relationship with school in the past will naturally be suspicious.

However, schools who can offer a failure-free method of known cost-effectiveness have inherent marketing advantages. They can say things like 'Come to school for 1 one-hour meeting and we will show you how at home in just 5 minutes a day for 5 days a week you can make your child a much better reader'.

Furthermore, they can say this confident that experience and research back them up, confident that the first graduates of the programme will spread the good news over the garden fences of the neighbourhood, confident that once some momentum builds the problem may be meeting all the demand.

They can also say this knowing that while the major marketing thrust may be in terms of parents helping children, which is highly socially acceptable, once a family has been empowered all kinds of other tutoring arrangements will spring up, truly embodying the full concept of Paired Learning.

In many cases the school will never know about these – they will involve that vast majority of low-literacy adults who hide their problem away and will never present themselves for a regular adult class. Paired Learning activities are a highly potent means of involving disaffected low-literacy adults. For many reading with their child is the only way of socially legitimizing reading books of low readability and infantile content. For many, 'helping' their child is their only motivation to read.

However, we will never reach all the families we would wish. Paradoxically, a school operating a successful parent-tutored Paired Learning programme can place the most disadvantaged children who are left out in a still worse position relative to those who are participating in the programme. This is of course where peer tutoring in school comes to the rescue.

Many teachers feel compelled to arrange alternative extra support for the most needy non-participant children, perhaps via volunteer adults coming into school or by giving up their own recess times to act as surrogate parents. Where any non-professionals are deployed as tutors, all the engineering considerations listed above apply. However, the organizational complexity of fixing up a reliable rota of substitute parents who are available often enough to actually make a difference to the child's attainment should not be underestimated. The teacher's own time is much too valuable to be used in this way.

Peer tutoring is the obvious answer. If appropriate methods are deployed, both tutees *and tutors* gain in attainment – the tutors 'learning by teaching'.

With an understanding of the basic principles of engineering for Paired Learning, you can begin to design projects and programmes specifically tailored to your own neighbourhood and classroom circumstances.

Part Four
Additional
Reproducibles

Part Four Section A
Paired Reading
Reproducibles

PRR4   Parent-tutored Paired Reading Planning Proforma

Context

Name of school: Age range:

Head Teacher:

Other teachers interested (name, position, responsibilities):

Project coordinator:

Size of school: Ethnic minorities:

Social advantage/disadvantage:

Size of catchment area and ease of access to school:

Other information about catchment area:

School reading standards – summary of survey data, etc.:

Reading teaching in the school:

Head Teacher's aims/wider problems:

Estimate of likely response of staff:

History of parental involvement with the school:

(a)   Social and fund-raising events:
(b)   Response to open evenings, etc.:

126

(c) Specific parental work in school:

(d) Contact with parents of likely target children:

Other comments re quality of school–community relationships:

Any likely problems:

Objectives

Target group (Tutees):

(a) Ages:

(b) Classes:

(c) Numbers:

(d) Ability range

Tutors:

(a) Natural parents:

(b) Parent volunteers:

(c) Staff volunteers:

(d) Other/Combination:

Project period (initial 'experimental' period):

Specific objectives:

1. _____

2. _____

3. _____

4. _____

5. _____

Materials

Free child selection/Guided child selection (how guided?)

(For each source of books below, note current and proposed access and loan recording system)

School library:

Classroom libraries:

Internal special collection:

Loan special collection:

Reading scheme (Basal readers):

School bookshop:

Community library:

Other/Special events:

Recruitment

First Introductory Letter:

- (a) with school report?
- (b) at/after open day?
- (c) timing?

Detailed invitation to meeting(s):

- (a) timing:
- (b) reply slip:

Reminder:

- (a) timing:
- (b) reply slip:

Consider:

1. Mail or child delivery?
2. Invitation in person to parents who come into school?
3. How to energize children to nag parents into coming?
   What advance build-up in school?
   Advance target group children meeting?
4. Telephone contact with parents?
5. Home visits for personal invitation?
6. Posters or public notices as well?
7. Local press publicity?

Training

Initial staff briefing/training

Time: Date: Duration:

Response/Reactions:

Who subsequently practised?

Training for tutors/tutees: Outline

One meeting or two?

Two-stage training or two parallel meetings?

With children?

Time(s):

Day(s) and date(s):

Transport provided?

   (a)   door-to-door?
   (b)   pick-up points?
   (c)   reimburse fares?

Place:

Position of electric points:
Access to TV/OHP?

Access to books for practice:
Books pre-chosen?

Practice space:

Crèche/child-minding/play space:

Arrangement for refreshments:
When?

Training for tutors/tutees: Detail

(For each component, specify if included and who will do it.)

Welcome:

Introduction:

'How Not To Do It': video or role play?

Talk: 'How To Do It':

Demonstration: Video/Live role play/Live child demo:

Practice (Name monitors):

Questions:

Talk on access to books/Home–School Records/Other follow-up:

Contracting (verbally/parents sign list/pair sign contract form):

Support and Monitoring

For children and parents

(a)   Home–school records:

                                  Cards, sheets or books?

Returned to: When?

(b)   Meetings in school:

Surgery or booster?

Individual or group or both?

With whom?

When?
How often?

(c)   Home visits:

By whom?   class teacher/specialist teacher/other
When?   school time/after school/evening
Frequency and pattern of visiting?
Can staffing be flexed to facilitate?
Reimbursement for travel/time possible?

For project staff

Mid-Project review

Time: Date:
Consultant to visit?

End-project review:

Time: Date:
Consultant to visit?

Feedback

Feedback meeting:

Individual: children present?

Group: children and parents together/separate/both?

Time(s):   Date(s):
Place:

Format: School perceptions, parent perceptions, child perceptions, evaluation
    results, client critique of training/follow-up, options for continuance (continue
    as now, continue with reduced frequency, continue with adjusted method, stop
    with view to later restart if required). Pair decision re continuance and record
    this. Certificates or other commendation for children.

Specifiy running order and who is to do what:

Evaluation

Reading tests/Assessments already in use in school:

Frequency: Time of year:

How far back does this data exist?

Methodology for project:

Standardized reading test(s):

Individual: Group:

Pre-/Post-/Baselined/Control Group?

Criterion-referenced reading assessments:
(IRIs, Cloze tests, word lists, etc.)

Other: Error frequency counts, rate, no. of books read, etc.

Attitudinal/Affective outcomes:

Structured teacher observations: Checklist or interview?

Structured child observations: Questionnaire or interview?

Structured parent observations: Questionnaire or interview?

Who and how to collate, analyse and disseminate evaluation results?

How to collect data for long-term follow-up?
6/12/18/24 months?

Was the project well organized?

Which of your objectives were met?
To what extent?

(1)

(2)

(3)

(4)

(5)

How would you improve it next time?

PRR5   Peer-Tutored Paired Reading Planning Proforma

A.   Context and Objectives

1   Objectives of project?
2   Support from colleagues/outside agencies?
3   Problems specific to the school?

B. Materials

1   Readability – how checked or controlled?
2   Choosing – who does, how freely?
3   Sources – reading scheme/school library/special collection/
    public library/home/etc.?
4   Access – as frequent as contact?

C. Selection and matching of children

1   Background factors – maturity, work habits, gender balance?
2   Age – same age or cross age?
3   Numbers – pairs to what total?
4   Reading ability – tutor/tutee differential?
5   Relationships – pre-existing?
6   Child preference – accept to what degree?
7   Spare tutors/ees – to cover absence?
8   Parental agreement – necessary?

D. Organization of Contact

1   Time – classtime/breaktime/both; fixed or various?
2   Place – classroom/leisure or play area/other?
3   Duration – 15, 20, 30 minutes?
4   Frequency – 3, 4, 5 x weekly?
5   Project period – 6, 8, 10 weeks?

E. Training

(a) Staff Training

(b) Child Training – Organization

1   Grouping – one group/two groups?
2   Venue – date/time/place?
3   A/V equipment – available/working?
4   Reading material – controlled for practice?
5   Practice space – check seats/noise levels

(c) Child Training – Content

1   Verbal instruction
2   Demonstration
3   Practice

4 Feedback
5 Coaching
6 Written instruction
7 Organizational details
8 Contracting

F. Support and Monitoring

1 Self-referral – to whom?
2 Observation – by teacher and/or child(ren)?
3 Self-recording – by tutor/tutees/both?
4 Discussion – group/individual, tutors/ees separate or not?

G. Feedback

1 Collation of information – variously for staff and children
2 Feedback to children – verbal/written/audio visual?
3 Feedback from children – group/individual; verbal/written?
4 Further decisions/Contracting – continue/reduce/change?

H. Evaluation

1 Current practice – ? continue to compare to baseline
2 Comparisons of project progress with:
  'normal' expectations/baseline/control group?
3 Normative testing – group/individual?
                    – accuracy/comprehension?
4 Qualitative testing – error analysis/IRI/Cloze/h-f words?
5 Subjective views – verbal or written, group or individual,
  tutors/ees/teachers?
6 Monitoring information – were organization/technique OK?

READING RECORD SHEET

Name: ....

DAY	BOOK CHOSEN	TIME SPENT	WITH WHOM	COMMENTS
Monday				
Tuesday				
Wednesday				
Thursday				
Friday				
Saturday				
Sunday				

Teacher's comment:

Signed:

Date:

PRR7   Dictionary of Praise

Introduction

In Reading Projects, the pairs often keep a diary or record of what they have done. The 'helper' of the pair is asked to write something each time about how well the 'reader' has done that day. It is best if the 'helper' can think of something good to write.

A lot of 'helpers' soon find it hard to think of new things to write. This little dictionary makes it easy. It has many ideas about words of praise to use. So if you get stuck for what to write, just read the dictionary together, till you find the words that seem right for the day. If the 'helper' has trouble choosing, ask the 'reader' for ideas of what would be right.

The words of praise are split into four groups. The first group is about 'Attitude' to reading – how the readers **feel** about reading, and if they have **liked** it. The second group is about 'Effort' – how hard the readers have **tried** with their reading. The third group is about 'Skill' – what the readers have **done** when reading which shows they are getting better. This is split into: (a) Accuracy – reading words **exactly right**, (b) Comprehension – **understanding** what you read, (c) Style – improvements in the **way** you read.

Readers often need to get better in Attitude and Effort before they get better in Skill – that is why praise is very important. The fourth group of praise words are shorter and more general – handy if you are in a rush.

Contents

(A)	ATTITUDE	– what you **feel** about reading
(B)	EFFORT	– how hard you **try** at reading
(C)	SKILL	– what you can **do** and **achieve** in reading
	1 Reading Accuracy	– reading words **exactly right**
	2 Reading Comprehension	– **understanding** what you read
	3 Reading Style	– the **way** in which you read
(D)	GENERAL	– 1 Getting better, showing improvement
		– 2 Good 'feeling' words, instant praise

(A)   ATTITUDE – what you **feel** about reading
    Words like 'very', 'really', 'more', 'increasingly', 'obviously',
    etc. can be added to many of these.

  Animated!
  Assured
  Believes in self as reader
  Cheerful re reading
  Couldn't put it down
  Couldn't wait to get going
  Didn't want to stop!
  Eager
  Enjoyed book in spite of difficulty
  Enjoyed every minute of reading
  Enjoyed him/herself
  Enjoys the reading tonic!
  Enthusiastic

Expects more of self
Fast-breeder reader
Hangs on every word
High-energy reading
Impatient to start
Interested
Keen
Less apprehensive
Likes the book
Lively reading
Loved the story
Motivation better
Optimistic re reading
Positive in approach
Prolific reader
A Reading dynamo
Reading more widely
Reading much more than before
A Reborn reader
Receptive
Renewed vigour in reading
A Restored reader
Self-reliant
Spontaneously asked to read
Takes pleasure in reading
Trying hard to please
Willing to read

(B) EFFORT – how hard you *try* at reading

Absorbed
Assiduous
Dedicated
Determined try
Doing a lot of hard work
Diligent
First long story read to the end
Good effort
Good try
He/she's framing him/herself
Indefatigable
Indomitable
Inexhaustible child
Intent
Keeps trying hard
Made a good effort
Maintaining
More willpower to succeed
Nearly read the whole chapter
Needs no nagging to read now
Non-stop reader!
Persevering
Persistence greater
Puts all his/her effort into it

Putting a lot of effort in today
Reading big words today
Really trying
Resolute
Staying the course well
Sustaining interest
Tackling hard words
Tenacious
Tireless
Tried very hard
Undaunted

(C.1) READING ACCURACY – reading words *exactly right*

Accurate (more)
Attention to punctuation better
Careful
Competent
Controlled reading
Did well to remember long words
Discriminates words better
Efficient
Errors fewer
Even less mistakes
Exact reader
Faultless
Fewer slips
Flawless
Getting the knack
Got a lot of difficult words right
Got no words wrong
Great improvement in pronunciation
Hardly any mistakes
Hardly got a word wrong
Hardly needed help
Immaculate
Impeccable
Infallible
Inspects words carefully
Little difficulty recalling hard words
Managed some tricky words
Memory better (for words)
Mistakes fewer
More accurate reading
No mistakes
Not a foot wrong
100 per cent
Only got one or two words wrong
Perfect
Precise reading
Proficient
Pronunciation better
Reads even complicated words
Reads long words straight off

Recalling better
Recollects well
Registers every word now
Retaining more words
Sharp-eyed reader
Skilful
Studies very carefully
Taking more care
Thorough
Two pages with no mistakes

(C.2) READING COMPREHENSION – *understanding* what you read

Asking more about meaning
Beginning to criticize books
Coherent when discussing
Conversation good
Delving into books
Discerning
Discussion good
Exploring books
Getting a feeling for words
Good comprehension
Good talk
Probes the meaning
Remembers 'story so far' better
Stopped a lot to discuss - good!
Taking more of the story in
Tries very hard to understand
Understanding more now
Understood difficult words

(C.3) READING STYLE – the *way* in which you read

Accomplished
Alert
Application better
Attention undivided
Beginning to correct him/herself
Careful
Clearer
Concentrating a lot better
Confident
Coping well
Determined
Diction better
Doubts self less
Dynamic reader
Excellent choice
Expects failure no longer
Expression coming along nicely
Expressiveness improved
Faith in self evident
Fluency improving
Fluent

Getting in tune
Getting onto a more difficult book
Getting settled now
Good attack!
Graceful reading
Graphic reading
Has a go at difficult words
Has stopped rushing
Hesitates much less
Keeping a steady flow
Keeping a steady pace
Lucid
Masterful
More expression
More variety in reading
Notices punctuation
Observant
Pacing better
Paying heed
Paying attention
Phrasing better
Professional
Reading more difficult words on own
Reading slower and better
Reads nearly all by self
Reads quite easily
Rhythmic
Ringing the changes in books
Sensitive reading
Signalling well
Smooth
Steadier
Stylish reading
Successful
Synchronized
Tackled the difficult words well
Taking notice
Takes the initiative well
Trusts own ability
Undistracted
Versatile
Vivid reading

(D.1) GENERALLY GETTING BETTER

Achieved a lot today
Advancing
Beneficial
Best ever
Best yet
Better
Better every minute
Blossoming
Breakthrough!

Catching on to reading
Change for the better
Classic reading
Coming on a bunch
Coming on great
Coming on a treat
Coped well
Developing
Did very well indeed
Doing well
Finding book quite easy
Forging ahead
Full marks
Getting better all the time
Getting better bit by bit
Getting on
Getting on to harder books
Good improvement
Good today
Great improvement
Has never read as well
Has never read better
Improved a bit more
Improved vastly
Improving all the time
Improving every day
Improving immensely
Improving rapidly
Improving slowly
Improving - very quickly indeed
Making great strides
Making headway
Mastering reading
Nearly as good as me
No problems
Overtaking me!
Picking it up well
Picking up
Productive reading
Progressing
Progressing in leaps and bounds
Purple patch
Radical change
Reading beautifully
Reading revival
Reformed reader
Rising reading star
Reading transfusion helping greatly
Showing promise
Showing results
Stretching ability
Taking off
Transformation
Turned the corner

Twigging what reading's about
Very competent
Vintage performance
Virtuoso performance

(D.2) GENERAL PRAISE – good *feeling* words

Absolutely brilliant today
Admirable
Ace
Apprentice doing well
Astounding
At his/her best today
Becoming a super reader
Began very well
Brilliant (brill)
Champion
Coach is pleased
Commended
Congratulations
Contented
Couldn't have done any better
Creditable
Delighted with him/her tonight
Definite improvement
Did very well
Doing nicely
Doing smashing
Eleven out of ten
Excellent
Fabulous
Fairly good
Fantastic
Fine
First rate
Gets carried away!
Going very well
Good
Good attempt
Good effort
Good little reader
Good progress
Good reading
Good start
Grand
Gratifying
Great
Happy session
Harmonious session
I am very pleased
I praised him/her a lot today
Ideal
Impressive
Jolly good today

Knockout
Lovely
Magic
Magnificent
Marvellous
Matchless
Miraculous
No problems
Out of this world
Pleased
Pleasing
Positive effect
Praiseworthy
Read better today
Reading very well
Read this book well
Satisfied
Second to none
Skilled
Smashing
So good I had to praise him/her many times
Sparkling reading!
Splendid
Stupendous
Super
Superb
Superfine
Superlative
Ten out of ten
Terrific (Triff)
The tops
Tip top
Top quality
Top seed reader
Tremendous today
Well done
Well read
Wizard
World beater
Wonderful
Wonderman/woman
Worthwhile
You are doing very well today
Zappy reading

Even with the help of this dictionary, you might want a change now and again.
Instead of writing, try putting stars:

★ average   ★★ good   ★★★ very good

or use smiley faces:

average  good  very good

or even points:

1 = average   2 = good   3 = very good

Some readers like to add up their stars or points each week, to see if they can get more the next week.

If the 'reader' does get more the next week, they might like a little 'treat' for doing so well. The 'helper' has done well, too, so they should get a treat also! But no cheating!

After reading for many weeks you might find that writing a comment just once or twice a week is enough. Do keep making a note of what you have read, though.

This book was made by looking through the diaries kept by lots of people in many different reading projects, and picking out the best words of praise they used. Thank you to all the children and adults who helped in this way.

PRR8   Paired Reading Technique Check List

Name: Date:

Check		Answer	Action
Books:	1 Variety of books?		
	2 Tutee choosing them?		
	3 Too hard or too easy?		
Time:	4 How long and often does the tutee read?		
	5 If a lot, does the tutee choose?		
	6 If not much, can someone else help?		
	7 If others help, how many others?		
Place:	8 Quiet?		
	9 Comfortable for both to see the book?		
	10 Ethos – close, warm and lively?		
Talk:	11 Both show interest in the book?		
	12 Both talk about content?		
	13 Tutee talks most?		
	14 Talk in Reading Together and Alone?		
New Ways:	15 No fussing about mistakes?		
	16 No breaking words up?		
	17 Pause for 4/5 seconds exactly?		
	18 Tutor repeats error words, correctly?		
	19 Tutee then repeats correctly?		
	20 Tutor praises a lot?		
	21 Praise given with feeling?		
Reading Together:	22 Reading Together exactly?		
	23 Flowing and lively, not jerky and flat?		
	24 Pointing to words – tutor or tutee?		
Reading Alone:	25 Tutee signals for Reading Alone?		
	26 Signal clear, easy and comfortable?		
	27 Tutor goes quiet straight away?		
	28 Tutor praises tutee for going alone?		
	29 Tutor praises during Reading Alone?		
	30 Pointing to words – tutor or tutee?		
	31 Tutor reads together again at error?		
	32 Reading Together till next signal?		
Notes:	33 Diary Record used?		
	34 Comments positive?		
	35 Comments made by teacher?		

PRR9a Paired Reading Evaluation Questionnaire
(for tutees)

Name:_____

Paired Reading	What was it like?

TICK WHICH IS TRUE FOR YOU

1 a. It was hard to get books   OR   b. It was easy to get books

2 a. It was easy to find time   OR   b. It was hard to find time

3 a. It was hard to find a good place to read OR   b. It was easy to find a good place to read

4 a. It was easy to learn to do   OR   b. It was hard to learn to do

5 a. I soon got fed up with it   OR   b. I liked doing it

6 a. The Record Sheet was a help   OR   b. The Record Sheet was no use

PAIRED READING HAS LED TO:

7 a. Not liking all kinds of reading   OR   b. Liking all reading better

8 a. Getting better at all kinds of reading   OR   b. No better at all kinds of reading

9 a. Getting on worse with each other   OR   b. Getting on better with each other

10 a. I want to go on doing Paired Reading   OR   b. I want to stop Paired Reading for now

11 a. I won't tell anyone about Paired Reading OR   b. I will tell other people about Paired Reading

12 Can you tell us one thing we can do to make Paired Reading better? Write what you think here:

PRR9b Paired Reading Evaluation Questionnaire
(for parents)

Name of child: _____

PLEASE TICK WHICH IS TRUE FOR YOU AS A RESULT OF PAIRED READING

A. Is your child:
(1) Reading more   about the same   Reading less
(2) Sticking to the same kind of book   about the same   Reading different kinds of book
(3) Understanding books more   about the same   Understanding books less

B. Is your child:
(4) Less confident in reading   about the same   More confident in reading
(5) More willing to read   about the same   Less willing to read
(6) Less interested in reading   about the same   More interested in reading
(7) Enjoying reading more   about the same   Enjoying reading less

C. When reading out loud, is your child:
(8) Making more mistakes   about the same   Making less mistakes
(9) Keeping a steadier flow   about the same   Stopping and starting more
(10) Reading in a lifeless, boring way   about the same   Reading with more life and expression

D. Is your child:
(11) Behaving better at home   about the same   Behaving worse at home
(12) Happier at home   about the same   Less happy at home

E. Are you going to:
(13) Stop Paired Reading, and perhaps start again later?   _____
      Go on doing Paired Reading, but only twice a week?   _____
      Go on doing Paired Reading 5 times a week?   _____
      Go on reading at home, but in a rather different way?   _____
Any other comments:

PRR9c   Paired Reading Evaluation Questionnnaire
(for peer tutors)

PAIRED READING   WHAT DO YOU THINK?

Name of Tutor: _____ Name of Tutee: _____

PLEASE TICK WHICH IS TRUE FOR YOU

A.   Is your tutee:
(1)   Reading more?   about the same?   Reading less
(2)   Sticking to the same kind of book   about the same   Reading different kinds of book
(3)   Understanding books more   about the same   Understanding books less

B.   Is your tutee:
(4)   Less confident in reading   about the same   More confident in reading
(5)   More willing to read   about the same   Less willing to read
(6)   Less interested in reading   about the same   More interested in reading
(7)   Enjoying reading more   about the same   Enjoying reading less

C.   When reading out loud, is your tutee:
(8)   Making more mistakes   about the same   Making less mistakes
(9)   Keeping a steadier flow   about the same   Stopping and starting more
(10) Reading in a lifeless, boring way   about the same   Reading with more life and
                                                                 expression

D.   Would you like to:

                                               CHOOSE UP TO THREE:
(11) Go on peer tutoring as often as now?   YES   _____
(12) Go on tutoring, but not so often?   YES   _____
(13) Go on tutoring, but with a different tutee? YES   _____
(14) Be tutored *yourself*, by someone better?   YES   _____
(15) Tutor reading, but in a different way?   YES   _____
(16) Tutor something else, like maths or spelling? YES   _____

Any other comments:

PRR9d Paired Reading Evaluation Questionnaire
(for teachers)

Name of child: _____

Please circle the answer indicated by your observations. Only indicate change if you feel it has occurred since Paired Reading started and is definite and significant.

A. *General*

Is the:

(1) Amount of reading done	less	more	same	not seen
(2) Width and variety of reading	more	less	not seen	same
(3) Comprehension of reading	same	not seen	more	less

B. *Attitude*

Is the:

(4) Confidence in Reading	not seen	same	less	more
(5) Willingness to Read	same	less	more	not seen
(6) Interest in Reading	more	not seen	less	same
(7) Pleasure in Reading	less	more	same	not seen

C. *Oral Reading*

Is:

(8) Accuracy	worse	better	same	not seen
(9) Fluency	better	same	not seen	worse
(10) Expressiveness	same	worse	better	not seen
(11) Pacing	not seen	better	worse	same

D. *Other*

Is:

(12) Concentration & Motivation generally	same	worse	not seen	better
(13) Behaviour generally	worse	not seen	better	same

(14) Any other significant changes (specify):

Thank you for giving your observations.

PAIRED LEARNING PROJECT

CERTIFICATE OF MERIT

FIRST CLASS

presented to

Signed

PRR11   Beyond Paired Reading

HOW DO YOU WANT TO PROGRESS?

Choose your option:

(1)   Stop Paired Reading for a rest (and perhaps start again later)
(2)   Go on with Paired Reading, but only twice a week
(3)   Go on with Paired Reading just as often as now
(4)   Go on to Stage 3 – Reading Mini-help
(5)   Go on to Stage 4 – Reading Silently
(6)   Go on to Stage 5 – Reading Solo

For more committed families and more competent readers

HOW TO GO ON FROM HERE

REMEMBER – LOTS OF PRAISE AT EVERY STAGE

1   PAIRED READING OCCASIONALLY

2   PAIRED READING REGULARLY

3   READING MINI-HELP

Tutee attempts all words Reading Alone;
Tutor gives correct example of error word only;
Tutee repeats correctly and continues Reading Alone.

4   READING SILENTLY

Pair both read each page silently sitting together;
Pair discuss and question about content at natural breaks.

5   READING SOLO

Pair discuss book;
Tutee Reads Alone silently sitting alone;
Tutee visits tutor at natural break for discussion/questions.
If the tutee tends to continue too long alone, a suitable natural break is agreed in advance.

REMEMBER:

If the tutee chooses a harder book, also choose a lower Stage.

Remember, the aim is *not* to get to Stage 5 and stay there.

Reading Together will still be necessary on very hard books!

Keep in touch with school about how you are doing.

PRR12   Overhead Masters – Paired Reading Method

WHAT TO READ

BOOKS, NEWSPAPERS OR MAGAZINES

FROM HOME, SCHOOL or LIBRARY

THE CHILD SHOULD CHOOSE THE BOOK

ANY STANDARD OF DIFFICULTY

LEAVE A BOOK WHENEVER YOU LIKE

TIME

LITTLE and OFTEN

5 MINUTES A DAY

5 DAYS A WEEK

FOR 6 TO 10 WEEKS INITIALLY

NOT MORE THAN 15 MINUTES A DAY UNLESS THE CHILD INSISTS

OTHER ADULTS AND OLDER CHILDREN CAN HELP – IN THE SAME WAY

152

PLACE

FIND THE QUIETEST PLACE YOU CAN

FIND SOMEWHERE COMFORTABLE

SIT SIDE BY SIDE – SO BOTH CAN SEE THE
BOOK EASILY

TALK

THE ADULT SHOULD SHOW INTEREST IN THE BOOK

TALK ABOUT THE PICTURES

TALK ABOUT THE STORY OR CONTENT

TALK AT A NATURAL BREAK (end of a paragraph or page)

BUT TALK TOGETHER – ADULT and CHILD MUST TALK and LISTEN EQUALLY

TALK TO MAKE SURE THE CHILD UNDERSTANDS

CORRECTION

WHEN THE CHILD GETS A WORD WRONG –
the ADULT says it CORRECTLY
(i.e. gives a perfect example)
the CHILD must SAY IT CORRECTLY
then you CARRY ON.

THIS CAN BE DONE QUICKLY, BEFORE THE
CHILD FORGETS WHAT THE START OF THE
SENTENCE WAS ABOUT.

BUT DON'T CORRECT TOO SOON –
GIVE THE CHILD 5 SECONDS
TO SEE IF THEY CORRECT IT THEMSELVES.

THE ADULT SHOULD:

– smile   – show pleasure

– say 'good'   – hug or squeeze

DO THIS VERY OFTEN
(as often as you can without it seeming silly)

PRAISE FOR:

GOOD READING OF HARD WORDS

READING A WHOLE SENTENCE OR PARAGRAPH RIGHT

PUTTING WORDS RIGHT BEFORE YOU DO

READING TOGETHER

THE ADULT AND THE CHILD <u>BOTH</u> READ ALL THE WORDS
OUT LOUD TOGETHER

DO NOT GO TOO FAST – MATCH SPEED TO THE CHILD

THE CHILD MUST READ EVERY WORD

SOME CHILDREN DON'T <u>LOOK</u> CAREFULLY ENOUGH

ESPECIALLY ON HARD READING
POINTING TO WORDS CAN HELP

READING ALONE

WHEN <u>YOUR CHILD</u> FEELS CONFIDENT ENOUGH, HE/SHE MIGHT WANT TO READ A BIT ALONE

AGREE ON A <u>SIGNAL</u> THE CHILD WILL MAKE FOR THE ADULT TO GO QUIET
(a knock, a nudge or a squeeze)

ON THE SIGNAL, THE ADULT GOES QUIET STRAIGHT AWAY AND THE CHILD READS OUT LOUD ALONE

WHEN THE CHILD MEETS A WORD THEY CAN'T READ CORRECTLY WITHIN 5 SECONDS –
CORRECT THE WORD
<u>AND THEN THE ADULT JOINS BACK IN
WITH READING TOGETHER</u>

WHEN THE CHILD AGAIN FEELS CONFIDENT ENOUGH TO READ ALONE, THE CHILD SIGNALS AGAIN, AND SO ON

PRR13   Overhead Masters – Research on Paired Reading

Data Type	Literature	School District
ALL STUDIES:	55 Projects	155 Projects
Accuracy Ratio Gains	4.22	3.27
Comprehension Ratio Gains	5.39	4.39
CONTROLLED STUDIES:	18 Projects	37 Projects
Accuracy Ratio Gains	P.R. 3.84 Control 1.56	P.R. 3.35 Control 1.99
Comprehension Ratio Gains Control 2.29	P.R. 4.57 Control 2.51	P.R. 4.55
FOLLOW-UP STUDIES:	5 Projects	17 Projects
(Ratio Gains) Short Term	Very various, some ‹1 but ›CG	Acc 2.01 Comp 2.32
Long Term	Full data not always cited	Acc 1.20 Comp 1.36

COMPARATIVE OUTCOMES OF PARENTAL INVOLVEMENT IN READING STUDIES

Programme Type	n studies	n studies	Rate of gain in reading accuracy
Paired reading Literature	60	1012	4.23 Comp n = 703 RG = 5.37
Paired Reading School District	155	2372	3.27 Comp n = 690 RG = 4.39
'Hearing'* Literature	14	290	2.53

* excluding Haringey & Belfield

PAIRED READING

SUBJECTIVE OPINIONS

<u>TEACHERS</u>   (475 IN 29 PROJECTS)

70% MORE CONFIDENT   (91% return rate)

67% MORE ACCURATE

59% MORE UNDERSTANDING

57% MORE ENJOYMENT   IN CLASS

<u>PARENTS</u>   (1068 IN 85 PROJECTS)

78% MORE CONFIDENT   (73% return rate)

71% MORE ACCURATE

68% MORE UNDERSTANDING

73% MORE ENJOYMENT   AT HOME

<u>CHILDREN</u>   (692 in 57 PROJECTS)

87% EASY TO LEARN TO DO   (72% return rate)

83% LIKED DOING IT

92% NOW LIKE READING MORE

95% ARE BETTER AT READING NOW

70% WILL GO ON WITH PAIRED READING

Reference

Topping, K. and Whiteley, M. (1990) Participant evaluation of parent-tutored and peer-tutored projects in Reading, *Educational Research* **32**(1), 14–32.

PAIRED READING
EFFECT SIZES

Literature	Mean E.S.	Range
(12 projects)	2.12	$+10.00 - +0.10$

L.E.A.	Mean E.S.	Range
(34 projects)	0.87	$+5.82 - -0.13$

The 2σ EFFECT

(Bloom)

Part Four Section B
Cued Spelling
Reproducibles

CSR3   Cued Spelling – How To Do It

Before You Start:

In most cases, the speller should be able to read a bit, know at least some names and sounds of letters, and be able to write so the tutor can read it. Those who can't write might still be able to do Cued Spelling by using a typewriter or computer, letter cards or plastic letters.

What You Need:

Pen or pencil, dictionary, piece of card, scrap paper, Cued Spelling flowchart, Cued Spelling Diary, Cued Spelling collecting notebook.

Time To Spend:

At least 5 words per day for 3 days of the week. Time spent each day varies with words chosen by speller and how well he or she does, but allow at least 15 minutes.

Technique   A   For each word   The 10 Steps

1.	CHOOSE WORD	Speller (tutee) chooses words, 5+ each day
2.	CHECK	Speller checks correct spelling in dictionary then writes word neatly in diary
3.	READ	(a) Read word Together
		(b) Reading Alone by speller
4.	CHOOSE CUES	Speller decides how to remember word by sounds, chunks, other mnemonics
5.	SAY CUES	Pair say Cues together
6.	DEMONSTRATE	Helper writes word as speller says Cues. Speller then checks word with diary
7.	CUED TRY	Speller writes word as helper says Cues
8.	SELF-CUE	Speller writes word while also saying Cues
9.	TEST	Speller writes word as quickly as possible
10.	READ	Speller reads word alone

Technique   B   Per Session   Speed Review

At the end of each day's session of the 10 Steps on 5 or more words, the helper (tutor) reads out all the day's words in a different order. The speller writes them as quickly and correctly as he or she can – then checks the words are spelled correctly with the Diary.

Technique   C   Per Week   Mastery Review

All the words for each week should be reviewed as in B (i.e. at least 3 lots of 5 words). If you have time, it is worth going over the whole Diary so far, or perhaps the last few weeks' words.

Technique   D   The 4 Points

1. Cover

From Step 6 to Step 9, the helper should make sure that any other examples of the word are covered up, so the speller can't just copy.

2. Check

Spellers always check their own try and should see their own mistakes when they check with the Diary. The helper does not point out mistakes – except when the speller checks but still doesn't notice a mistake. The Spelling Diary *must* only have words spelled correctly in it.

3. Mistakes

From Step 6 to Step 9, at every Step any words written wrongly should be well crossed out by the speller.

For any mistake in the 10 Steps, go back to the Step **before** and do it again.

For any mistake in Speed Review (B), go over the 10 Steps again for that word. A different Cue could be used at Step 4.

For any mistake in Mastery Review (C), decide for yourselves what you want to do about it. You might want to carry that word forward to the next week.

Helpers should not moan about wobbly writing. Where a written word is hard for the helper to read, the helper should ask the speller to write it again.

4. Praise

The helper praises (says 'good' or 'well done' and smiles) the speller at least for:

(A)   The speller putting his or her own mistake right before check with example;
(B)   Getting each word right at Step 9 TEST;
(C)   Getting each word right at Speed Review (B) or Mastery Review (C).

CSR4   Mnemonic Strategies

RULES – some spellings do follow logical rules (like 'i before e, except after c' – which most people remember). The learner may be helped by rules like this, but (a) make sure you've got them right, and (b) keep them simple and few in number.

WORD IN WORDS – just breaking words up into bits like syllables helps us to remember them, but if you can break them up into smaller words that mean something, it's even easier to remember them. Words like shep/herd, care/taker and water/fall are like this.

FRONTS AND BACKS – quite a lot of words have the same sort of start or finish. Starts and finishes can be looked at closely in a set of words that start or finish the same. Starts (like 'sta-', 'pre-', 'un-') are often not as hard as finishes (like '-tion', '-ate', '-ous', '-ght').

FAMILIES – words which have the same fronts and backs can be put in groups or families. Sorting out the words into families can be a game, perhaps even with a little prize for the winner. You can do this with words that have the same middles, too. You might think of other ways of sorting words into families or categories.

MAKE A PICTURE – if you can make up a picture in your mind about a word, this will help you remember it. (Like thinking up a picture of two people getting married (wed) on a Wednesday to remind you how to spell the name of that day.) Some of your mind pictures or 'visual images' will seem really silly – but this is good, because if they are funny you will remember them better.

RELATIONS – two words that look different can still sometimes be related (or 'associated') in some way. If you can relate a word you don't know to one you do know, you then might remember them together – right! Like:

> 'b **icy** cle' – 'fridge'.

But the learner must be able to remember the second word (e.g. fridge) easily. It is usually easier to remember there is a link between words than remembering there is not a link or relationship between words.

SHRINK AND GROW – with some words, you can remember a short difficult bit of it or just some initials for each part, like 'par' in 'separate'. Often it helps to 'grow' the initials into new words, to give you a saying or rhyme to remember.

> Like: b / e /   a /   u / tiful
> big elephants aren't ugly
>
> n   e   c   e   s   s   ary
> 1 collar   and   2 socks

FIX AND STRETCH MEANING – it helps if we really understand what those difficult words mean. The learner might choose them because they seem interesting, but talking about the full and exact meaning and use for a while will make the word even more interesting, and help fix it in the learner's mind.

FUNNIES – as much as you can, work jokes and other silly and comic things into what you do with Cued Spelling. Funny things are much more likely to be remembered.

RHYME AND RHYTHM – rhyme is very good for helping you remember, like in 'i before e except after c'. If finding a rhyme is too difficult, try to get some rhythm into the mnemonic so it is easier to say. You could even try singing some of the words!

HIGHLIGHT – we only usually get one bit of a difficult word wrong. Try highlighting the difficult bits with colours (perhaps green for easy bits, red for hard bits). Or just use capital letters or underline: e.g. stationEry

Different learners must find out by trying which of these ways works best for them. Different learners will find different ways better. The helper must not push the learner into a particular way, especially not into the way that feels easiest to the helper!

Your Cued Spelling will not do much good if the learner doesn't get lots of practice with writing as well. To become a better speller, you need to practise writing, wherever you are. The learner needs to write shopping lists, leave notes and messages, write letters and requests, and so on. Find reasons to write and audiences for writing.

This list may give you some ideas, but helpers often have good ideas which are too complicated for learners to remember. It's better if learners think up their own ideas, if they can. They will have to remember them quickly and easily if they need to use the difficult word when writing, so the ideas must be 'short and sweet'.

Remember:

1. KEEP IT SIMPLE
2. LET THE LEARNER DO WHAT'S EASY FOR HIM OR HER
3. FIND LEARNERS REASONS TO WRITE

CSR5   Mnemonic Ideas

Sometimes Cued Spellers think of really clever and imaginative ways of remembering spellings. These mnemonics often seem very strange, but they make sense to the speller who thought them up! It is very difficult to teach someone how to think up mnemonics, because one that works for one person may not work for another – you have to think up your own, that are memorable for you.

Some mnemonics that were thought up by 7- to 9-year-old children are printed below. These are only intended as examples to give you an idea of what can be done – don't think that they will necessarily be any good for you to use yourself.

1. **beau**tiful   – big elephants aren't ugly
                           (in fact, they are beautiful)

(mnemonics may only refer to that part of the word that the speller finds difficult)

2. **because**   – big elephants cannot always use small escalators
3. **Canada**   – Cannonballs are nice and dirty articles
4. **caught**   – cats always use great heavy toilets
5. **dictionary**   – names: DIC   TION   ARY
                       (Dick and Harry shun the third person!)
6. **ghost**   – ghosts hate oranges, sausages, tea
7. **graphs**   – giant rabbits are pretty hopeless skippers
8. **lasagne**   – little apes sit and gobble nuts energetically
9. **piece**   – a **pie**ce of **pie**
10. **professor**   – 1 frog and 2 snakes
11. **question**   – queens undress everywhere so they're in our news
12. **special**   – some people eat crabs in a lavatory

Lots of these mnemonics are quite funny – no teacher could have thought of them! – and some were illustrated. This helped the spellers to remember. Some seem very complicated, but remember that in Cued Spelling you don't have to be able to read or write down the mnemonic Cues, only be able to say them. In the long run you will remember the word after you have forgotten the Cue. But don't make the Cues **too** complicated!

CSR6   Abbreviated Cued Spelling Procedure

1   CHECK DICTIONARY TOGETHER

2   SPLIT WORD UP

3   HELPER SAYS BITS, WRITES WORD

4   SPELLER SAYS BITS AND WRITES

5   SPELLER WRITES WORD FAST

6   RE-TEST ALL WORDS EVERY WEEK

A   SPELLER AND HELPER CHOOSE WORDS

B   COVER OTHER TRIES

C   SPELLER CHECKS OWN TRY

D   IF WRONG, GO BACK A STEP

E   HELPER PRAISES

CSR7a Cued Spelling Evaluation Questionnaire (for tutees)

TICK WHICH IS TRUE FOR YOU.

1 a. It was easy to find time _____
   b. It was hard to find time _____

2 a. It was hard to find a good place to do it _____
   b. It was easy to find a good place _____

3 a. It was easy to learn to do _____
   b. It was hard to learn to do _____

4 a. It was hard to think of good words _____
   b. It was easy to think of good words _____

5 a. It was easy to think of good Cues _____
   b. It was hard to think of good Cues _____

6 a. I don't feel any happier about spelling _____
   b. I feel happier about spelling now _____

7 a. I do better at spelling tests now _____
   b. I am just the same as ever at spelling tests _____

8 a. I am just the same at spelling when writing _____
   b. I do better at spelling when writing now _____

9 a. I can put more mistakes right by myself now _____
   b. I don't put any more mistakes right by myself _____

10 a. I didn't get enough praise from my helper _____
    b. My helper gave me enough praise _____

11 a. I liked doing Cued Spelling _____
    b. I soon got fed up with Cued Spelling _____

12 a. I won't tell anyone about Cued Spelling _____
    b. I will tell other people about Cued Spelling _____

(Choose one answer and tick it.)

13 I will:
    a. stop Cued Spelling and perhaps start again later _____
    b. go on doing Cued Spelling but not so often _____
    c. go on doing Cued Spelling as often as now _____
    d. do spelling work, but in a different way _____

Any other comments: Name: _____

THANK YOU FOR TELLING US WHAT YOU THINK

CSR7b Cued Spelling Evaluation Questionnaire
(for tutors)

TICK WHICH IS TRUE FOR YOU.

1   a. It was easy to find time   _____
    b. It was hard to find time   _____

2   a. It was hard to find a good place to do it   _____
    b. It was easy to find a good place to do it   _____

3   a. It was easy to learn to do   _____
    b. It was hard to learn to do   _____

4   a. It was hard for the tutee to think of good words   _____
    b. It was easy for them to think of good words   _____

5   a. It was easy for the tutee to think of good Cues   _____
    b. It was hard for the tutee to think of good Cues   _____

6   a. The tutee seems no happier about spelling now   _____
    b The tutee seems happier about spelling now   _____

7   a. The tutee puts more mistakes right on their own now   _____
    b. The tutee doesn't put any more right on their own   _____

8   a. I found it difficult to praise my tutee   _____
    b. I gave my tutee lots of praise   _____

9   a. I liked doing Cued Spelling   _____
    b. I soon got fed up with Cued Spelling   _____

10 a. I think my own spelling got better as well   _____
    b. I think my own spelling is just the same   _____

11 a. I won't tell anyone about Cued Spelling   _____
    b. I will tell other people about Cued Spelling   _____

(Choose one answer and tick it.)

12 I want to:
    a. stop Cued Spelling and perhaps start again later   _____
    b. go on doing Cued Spelling but not so often   _____
    c. go on doing Cued Spelling as often as now   _____
    d. do spelling work, but in a different way   _____

Any other comments: Name: _____

THANK YOU FOR TELLING US WHAT YOU THINK

CSR8 Overhead Masters – Research on Cued Spelling

Emerson (1988)
Scoble (1988)
Brierley *et al.* (1989)
Harrison (1989)
Scoble (1989)
Oxley and Topping (1990)
France *et al.* (1993)
Watt and Topping (1993)

BRIERLEY et al. (1989)

SAME-AGE RECIPROCAL PEER TUTORING

WITH 3 WHOLE CLASSES, 9–10 YEARS

WEEKLY ROLE CHANGE

TEST GAIN 0.65 YEARS in 6 WEEKS

MASTERY REVIEW 80%

84% OF CHILDREN FELT BETTER SPELLERS

OXLEY AND TOPPING (1990)

CROSS-AGE PEER TUTORING

7–9-YEAR-OLDS

SELF IMAGE SCORES UP c.f. CONTROLS

SOCIAL BENEFITS AND GENERALIZATION

MASTERY REVIEW 66%

BIG TEST GAINS, BUT CONTROLS ALSO

SUBJECTIVE FEEDBACK VERY POSITIVE

FRANCE et al. (1992)

PARENT TUTORED AT HOME

8–10-YEAR-OLDS

TEST GAIN 0.51 YEARS IN 6 WEEKS

(CONTROL GROUP 0.18 YEARS)

74% BETTER AT SPELLING NOW (CHILD VIEWS)

85% HAPPIER ABOUT SPELLING (CHILD VIEWS)

WATT AND TOPPING (1993)

CUED SPELLING vs TRADITIONAL SPELLING HOMEWORK

PARENT vs PEER TUTORING

?GENERALIZATION TO FREE WRITING

TEST GAINS > 2× 'NORMAL' RATES

AND 4× THE PROGRESS OF 'HOMEWORK' GROUP

CUED SPELLING FREE WRITING IMPROVED MORE THAN TRADITIONAL SPELLING HOMEWORK

MASTERY REVIEW 93%

PARENT TUTORING = PEER TUTORING

Part Four Section C
Paired Writing
Reproducible

PWR2   Paired Writing Evaluation Questionnaire

TICK ANY BOX WHICH IS TRUE.

1   a It was easy to find time
    b It was hard to find time

2   a It was easy to learn to do
    b It was hard to learn to do

3   a I liked doing Paired Writing
    b I soon got fed up with Paired Writing

How well did Paired Writing work compared to writing alone?

Answer for both yourself and your partner if you can:

Did you see:

	Tutor	Tutee

4   More and better ideas?
5   Better organization and structure
6   More varied and exact words?

7   Better grammar?
8   Better spelling?
9   Better punctuation?

10   More interest?
11   More confidence?
12   Better concentration?

13   I want to:

    a go on doing Paired Writing but not so often
    b go on doing Paired Writing as often as now
    c do all writing on my own
    d do writing in pairs but in a different way

(If you ticked d, what would the other way be? Write about it below.)

Your Name: _____ Tutor or Tutee? _____

Any other comments:

THANK YOU FOR TELLING US WHAT YOU THINK

Index

PR = Paired Reading; CS = Cued Spelling; PW = Paired Writing